a season of orders!
(the weird ways of military regimes)

D1350874

a season of orders!
(the weird ways of military regimes)

'safe adewumi

Spectrum Books Limited
Ibadan
Abuja • Benin City • Lagos • Owerri

Spectrum titles can be purchased on line at
www.spectrumbooksonline.com

Published by
Spectrum Books Limited
Spectrum House
Ring Road
PMB 5612
Ibadan, Nigeria
e-mail: admin1@spectrumbooksonline.com

in association with
Safari Books (Export) Limited
1st Floor
17 Bond Street
St Helier
Jersey JE2 3NP
Channel Islands
United Kingdom

Europe and USA Distributor
African Books Collective Ltd
The Jam Factory
27 Park End Street
Oxford OX1, 1HU, UK

First published, 2003

ISBN: 978-029-431-7

Printed by Printmarks Ventures, Ososami, Ibadan

dedication

Not to the tirade experts against Nigeria from abroad. But to those who, with their consistent verbal salvoes, displayed a strong and genuine belief in a virile democratic Nigeria; and who, without violence, patiently waited for an opportunity for the present democracy that must no longer slip for flimsy reasons.

Dedicated principally to the *Almighty God.* To the Talba of Bauchi, Dr. Ibrahim Tahir who prefaced my first work; *'Points of Disorder'* with the words *"Nigerians are looking forward to what is coming next".* And to Professor Jerry Gana, the Honourable Minister for Information and National Orientation who expressly stimulated another work with the encouraging marketing of my first satire on national politics.

To my entire family who share the joy of the first work and encouraged me to move another step. Particularly my daughters, *'Nifemi and Jemiseye,* who offered their semester breaks for script compusetting. To the Nigerians who went through the gulag of military dictatorship, harassed with volleys that missed or got their targets, separated from loved ones and ceaselessly hunted in exile, I dedicate.

foreword

Historians record history, while fiction writing is part of the preoccupation of literary artists. Although history is not fiction, fiction can be based on history. This book, *a season of orders*, is in effect, a work of fiction which is based on history. It has chronicled the history of Nigeria with emphasis on her fifteen years under a prolonged phase of military dictatorship. In this regard, it may be considered a sort of 'contemporary Nigerian history' preserved and narrated to us in the form of a fiction. This form of history does not require evidence. In any case, for those of us who lived and experienced the tragedy of those horrible fifteen years of military dictatorship, we may never really require additional evidence to prove to ourselves what happened to us. For, it is, what we may call, a life-long bitter experience. As a matter of fact, only very few Nigerians can dare say that what happened in the past fifteen years did not happen. Neither could they afford to even forget what happened!

One of the most fascinating aspects of this book is its attempt to expose the multi-faceted nature of the impact of military rule in Nigeria. It looks at the military, first, as an institution facing crisis; the most important aspects being the erosion of professionalism and the difficulty in which military officers found themselves on the issue of loyalty to constituted political authority, especially in the case of a military regime.

a season of orders has been able to capture this difficulty by illustrating it with the case of an officer who reported a military coup plot in a military regime to his senior officer. But instead of being commended, he was promptly locked up. It did not occur to the 'loyal officer' that his superior officer was the one spearheading the coup until he was announced as the new Head of State. When next a coup plot was being hatched, he did not report it to his superior officer and the coup plot was eventually uncovered by the military regime in power. The unfortunate officer was again promptly arrested, investigated, tried, convicted and executed. However, shortly after his execution, it was discovered that this officer was not involved in the coup plot. But it was then too late to do anything.

The then government hurriedly organised some financial compensation for his family. Furious and frustrated, the officer's wife rejected the offer. It did not end there. She also resolved that none of her kids would join any of the armed forces.

This disorientation of the military ultimately made officers become preoccupied with jostling for political positions like those of Governor, Minister and Head of State. The question of becoming a General or a Marshal was secondary, hence the reasons for persistent coups and counter coups.

While military rule disoriented the military as an institution, it discredited the civil society. The case of a University Lecturer with some modicum of radicalism and fervent advocacy for social reform was used to illustrate the hollowness of armchair criticism. Here was a holder of a doctoral degree in political science, vocal in advocating for reforms and justice but who readily accepted the appointment offered to him by another military junta as Information Minister. Of course, his job was to sell and justify to the public, all the misdemeanour of the military junta. And this was at a time when 'all the tiers of education in the country had sunk into the doldrums.'

The press too was not left behind. The media became irrational in reporting and assessing events, and this had profound negative impact on the image of the country in the eyes of the international community. This negative impact of the media was such that many of them seemed to have lost confidence in the continued existence of the country. This was evident in their negative coverage and cover captions like; 'It is Finished', 'Break Up Now' and 'This Country is Gone'.

The nation's economy also experienced a downturn. The result was massive unemployment, corruption, poverty, high-rate of inflation, social dislocation and general hopelessness in the society. Even the elite resorted to buying fairly-used cars, called *Tokunboh*, as they could no longer afford new cars.

Then came the turn of the politicians who 'hardly thought right, talked right' or behaved right about the democratic way forward'. They welcomed every military regime, accepted political appointments and fat contracts and cried out only when they felt unfairly treated. This set of people moved from one transition to another, therefore creating room for an effective entrenchment of diarchy in the country. Thirsty for power, they accepted everything from the military, without hesitation, including government created parties. And so when the time for presidential elections came, close friends of the military president lined-up to contest. Consequently, the election was cancelled and crisis erupted. It ultimately led to another coup.

Much as this book is a work of fiction, it nevertheless tries to capture the social and political reality of our country in the fifteen years of uninterrupted military rule, a reality that cannot be disputed. That is what a serious work of fiction does.

M.D. Yusufu
Lagos, Nigeria

introduction

Human beings naturally wish to be praised and adulated for their little ideals and perfections, but they very often resent corrections for their huge inadequacies and absurdities. This propensity is latent, not only in the physical make-up of *'beings'*, but also in their outlooks and callings.

This latest work is bound, in my mind's eye, to be considered in that light by some individuals and groups largely arising from their ignorance of the ideals of correction and the virtue of identifying the tremendous realignment of opportunities offered by mistakes.

Again, this latest work from the stable of *'Orders'* is meant to be a deterrent work for everyone, group and particularly, individuals attempting to learn a little lesson in their resolve to play *GOD* in our ethnically diverse nation with a politically restless military, constantly pointing the bayonet at our common treasury.

This is a pure work of art on the pitfalls and candourless nature of military politics which is used more for selfish acquisition and group, institutional and national retardation. It bears no particular reference to anyone, living or dead. It is a *Note of Lesson* containing tutorials for everyone that cares. I equally appeal for understanding from any reader who may view, as offensive, some usage of the military lingua franca: the *pidgin*. The *khaki* is not complete without it.

By way of acknowledgement, I sincerely appreciate the immeasurable relevance of all those who have authored various works already in print. Even when we can see, hear and record by ourselves, past works on diverse subjects are still relevant for a successful assemblage of facts as contained in a work of this nature.

If *Carlos Fuentes,* the Argentine writer is right, then there is no orphan book! No literary work is without a parent in various degrees of relevance! I therefore acknowledge all works and records from where memory was re-charged for this assemblage.

To be deep enough to generate controversy, stimulate debate and be generally appreciated therefore, a piece of political satire like this one cannot afford to be parentless! I acknowledge the richness of its ancestors, by which I mean, all previous essays before it.

prince 'safe adewumi
february 2002

"Today, fear runs in the land... But if we can get to the stage where we can encourage everybody, despite age and status, to criticise openly, express their minds and make suggestions freely, then we are getting nearer to democracy."

Sheila Solarin
The Guardian Personality Interview

"Happily, we played a role in bringing peace to Liberia and stability to Sierra Leone by bringing back a deposed elected president. This confirms that the military and the security forces are capable of democratisation. In all the. consultations I had, one thing is clear and that is; Nigerians want democracy and this we intend to do. We are resolved to handover power to a democratically elected government in this country... and you must be careful of those that will weaken your resolve for democracy."

General Abdulsalami Abubakar
Nigeria's Former Head of State addressing military officers, 18th and 19th August, 1998 in Ibadan and Enugu respectively.

order one, rule one

"...when there are no wars to fight, we create one by ourselves"

It all began at the officer's mess of the 302 Regiment at Lishi, a northern city of considerable military concentration, several hundred kilometres to the nation's capital. It was an ideal location for such an elite corps in the country's military set-up, far thrust into the jungle with enough grazing ground for the MP5 sub-machine guns and the cluster of highly equipped and modern T-12 tanks in their weekly manoeuvre.

Carefully chosen and well tested, the regiment looked close to unsung heroes in their former units. The task was to master their terrain with neurotic ability and protect the growing wealth accruing from the oil sector, a unique assignment besides the traditional role of protecting the nation.

To imagine a high degree of comfort was a forgone conclusion from the inception of the barracks project at Lishi. The gargantuan facilities became spoilers with vast processional avenues serving as parade grounds. Daises for salute were numerous. Well laid-out living quarters for officers and other ranks edged off deep recessing culverts that clearly demarcated the asphalt surfaced dual-carriage ways from the lawns. Recreation was wide, in line with the military tradition of having the boys *'in top form'*.

Lishi was definitely a clear world from the high-class dwellings of the kobo-pinchers in the capital city of Lapas, and very much envied by workers clustering in the ghetto-like government quarters. The streak of snobbery and the enormous conceit in all men of the 302 regiment was therefore a creation by people who never envisaged it. Lishi became a breeder of petrels in politics and military life, where a degree of unrelenting harshness was perpetually infused into the officers.

On the antiseptic white tiles in the billiard room of the mess that evening, two of such officers were seated, playing cards. It was a close-up session. The stillness of the night made all card movements audible. Suddenly the door opened with a screech, diverting the attention of Captain Sanni Jibo and Major Samson Bellah from their object of pleasure.

"Enemy or friend?" they raged at the intruder in fierce tones for daring the diversion that overturned the pin-drop silence in the room.

"One friend, one foe Sir!" the barman barked out, assuming a stone-dead posture as he stood at attention, an oak-like six footer in French suit.

"*Sirs! This man, he say he be Lieutenant Riwa. He won comot for mess by force. I tell am say one Major, one Captain still dey mess. By order, he no fit go if officer still dey mess Sir. He dey disturb efferyone. Das why I carry am come, Sir!*"

"So, barman, you are the friend and the Lieutenant is the enemy? All right, I Captain Jibo command that the friend be at ease and advance one step while the enemy stays at attention!" The barman and Lieutenant Riwa both advanced one step and eased off attention.

"See the foolish man committing another offence!" Captain Jibo raged again.

"Sorry Sir, I am not an enemy to anybody here. Besides, the barman didn't carry me here as he alleged. I am not disabled. I walked into this room by myself. The issue is that I came to the mess with only a hundred naira to cool down after today's exhausting bush exercise. I finished my beer before you came in about two and a half hours ago. The idea is to have a bottle to lure me into sleep after the exhaustion. Now, Sir, the beer is gone completely with urine, no going home and no money to call for another bottle.

"Unswerving loyalty to military rules and traditions kept me waiting till this hour before deciding to approach you for permission to fall out. I was ..."

"Shuut - up!"

"No, Captain, let him continue. I am interested in that young man. He sounds brand new with uncorrupted military software kicking in him". Major Bellah cuts in, displaying all manner of interest in the discovery of a man of such courage and enviable verbal disposition.

"O.K. Oga say make you talk."

"Nothing to talk again, Sir. But if I cannot move out because officers are still around, I think the officers must make my forced stay enjoyable. Afterall you can ..."

"What is your name?" Major Bellah asked.

"Lieutenant G.S. Riwa, Sir."

"When did you join the army?"

"Seven years ago, Sir. Commissioned four years back and deployed to 302 Regiment shortly after."

"G.S. Riwa you say?" Major Bellah asked again. "Tell me more about yourself."

"Sir, I trained at the Rivside Depot. There, I won the commander's sword for the best student in pistol firing techniques. At the regiment, here in Lishi, I lead a platoon for a weekly bush exercise. I conduct lessons in advanced gun slinging and firing over the shoulder at targets sighted through the mirror with pinpoint accuracy. Sir, without any intent of personal adulation, I have developed obsessive and prodigious appetite for efficient weapon handling. I love challenges and I make myself available easily for risky missions. My unit commander knows that, and as for duty hours, I love them long and painful. That is the military!"

Major Bellah was puzzled at the credentials. He emptied his almost forgotten glass of beer, adjusted himself to a more convenient position on the couch. He addressed the barman first:

"You can fall-out, *Serg*. Give beer to all the boys still hanging there. After that, I permit them to go. It is almost midnight. We will let you know when we are set to leave."

"Yes Sir!"

"Now, Riwa. Lieutenant Riwa, you sound as a whiplash officer. You impress me as a promising officer with an IQ above 110 and the ability to stay cool and calculated under the daunts and panics associated with the military. You must use your ability to the advantage of your country. Are you prepared?"

"Very well, Sir. I have been looking forward to such an opportunity since I speak the three main national languages fluently. But Sir, I am thirsty, can I order a bottle?"

"Go ahead Lieutenant. Permission granted!"

Lieutenant Riwa quickly dashed to the bar and wasted no time re-appearing with a bottle, half full, firmly clutching to a glass with a settling foam of beer bubbles, indicating that the first cup was gulped down hurriedly.

"So quick?" Captain Jibo queried.

"Everything must be military Sir. I am always on the offensive, Sir. I don't engage in defensive actions. I am a fighting man, a man who would kiss his tearful wife goodbye and put on his uniform to go to war!" Riwa bellowed back in what is more of self-conceit than force.

"There is going to be a revolution in this country." Major Bellah opened up again, turning to captain Jibo to seek his approval to continue as he puts the card on the table. Captain Jibo nodded consent.

"There is going to be a revolution. Our people are politically very hollow and empty. Financial madness is assuming a proportion that can no longer be placated by sheer indifference, threat or persuasion. Our politicians are ruling without direction because of vanity. I am not a politician or a university lecturer, but a search through history in recent months has convinced me that revolution is the only answer to problems created by vanity in any country.

"You see, our institutions are no longer humane and just. As such, our people too are no longer human. Independence has taken the wind out of our sail and rocked our boat. We nurtured the political wolves now ravaging our flock in their well-laid-out green pastures. There is chaotic indiscipline, and reckless political power, used for its own advantage, has overtaken our decency. We can do better than we are doing presently if we are not indisciplined and restricted by thugs who deceive and pretend to be politicians. We should stop being foolish and realise that our qualities and national potentials have been lost into the ethnic parallelograms into which we have been dragged by people in flowing *babarigas....*"

He paused to seek a fresh mandate to continue and to give Lieutenant Riwa a seat and to share the card table. Riwa relaxed his fingers by placing his empty glass and bottle on the table.

"I am confused, Sir," he mused remorsefully.

"Yes, that's what the government is capable of bringing to everyone. Confusion! People in this country have been thoroughly confused, not only at the rudderless ship of state, but also at the very idea of even calling for self-government. Politics is everywhere: religion, education, social sector, civil service, economy and even the military. The confusion has also blinded the military from learning about how similar situations were handled in other countries. The basic fact believed by Jibo and myself is that failure will not be failure if it cannot banish illusions and show the way to a plan.

"Part of that plan is what is now unfolding and for which you are now an accomplice.

"Lieutenant Riwa, there is going to be a *coup-d'état* and we want someone like you to be involved. The government of this country must be overthrown, if we must move forward," Major Bellah concluded as he proceeded to pull out his pistol with rage; suggesting that a coup plan, once discussed will not accommodate disclosures or back-outs. Hence, an oath was necessary.

"Oga, I see coups as a military adventure of less glory and clear danger. How do we avoid bloodshed, sectional protection, casualty, misinterpretation of intentions, failures and, above all, superpower condemnation and isolation?" the young Lieutenant queried.

"Already, we have a handful of volunteers highly skilled in speed and decisive moves peculiar to our own military terrain. If resistance is low, the use of firearms will be superfluous, thereby limiting casualties to an acceptable level.

"The armoury here is open to us, courtesy of Captain Jibo, and we will not abort a noble cause just because we plan to prevent military or civilian casualties. This is a country of over a hundred million people, and there is a ratio of that number that is acceptable as a loss in military operations. Besides, execution is being carefully approached to enable it have a national spread. A new government must start on a clean slate. Only then can the big powers be favourably disposed to our cause. We must be mindful that we are in the best position ourselves to solve any problem threatening our territorial integrity.

"We must not allow the danger of offending a super-power to be a limiting factor. Posterity will not forgive us if we treat, with uncanny privilege, the fear of letting the nation sink deeper into stagnation and backwardness just because ethnic groupings must not be offended and a fragile unity must be maintained. There is no going back! Neither the thought of failure, imprisonment, execution nor a pardon and eventual discharge into poverty must stand in our way!" Major Bellah concluded and waited for response.

"I see! I see, Sir. But..."

"*But* me no *but* Lieutenant. The butt and barrel of that gun is what matters now. Your allegiance first before you talk. You are already in the plan by merely listening. A disclosure of the plan means clear injury to the service of everyone. Your oath please!"

"*Ah, Oga! You wear mufti and you carry weapon come mess! Sir, nah offence o!*"

"Lieutenant, forget that. Just give me your oath!"

Lieutenant Riwa kissed the barrel of the *barretta* pistol twice, pledging allegiance to topple the government of his country, a treason.

"I say on oath here, Sir, that I commit my life to this cause. What we are doing now is to lay the bedrock of a small success, capable of projecting our country to greater heights in social, economic and political development. I have never been anybody's hatchet man. I do a job when I feel convinced as I now feel and my signing-up is not to ensure that there are no mistakes at the cost of having no successes. The youth of this nation and the junior officers particularly are aware that our leaders daily seek refuge in extravagant illusions. Ostentatious oddities stare us in the face because of the great deluge of human stupidity. I am ready to serve, Sir, especially in the training of the assault boys."

"Good of you, Lieutenant." Captain Jibo responded after carefully listening for over an hour. His fluent accent was fascinating in that dead of the night. The mess looked so brilliantly white, the polished wood and gleaming chrome, which gave it the look of an art gallery, seemed to be the only listeners to a *fellow countrymen* slogan.

"My friend, when God decides to get involved in a nation or a person, allegiance becomes necessary. God has endorsed this plan. Our duty, therefore, is to keep the confusion and casualties as low as possible. Plans have to be carefully worked out, men properly selected and the time accurately chosen. The D-day has been fixed for April 1, an all fools' day. The country has been divided into northern and southern commands, to be co-ordinated by two Majors and two Captains.

"For the northern command, Major Bellah and myself are in charge. We will use our men to hit the northern regional capital of Kadah. Major S.O. Boo and Captain T. John, two tough officers with proven endurance and considerable intellect in urban military assaults, are to take charge of the national capital.

"Final ratification of plans is expected in a fortnight at a meeting billed for *Ekikun*, a holiday resort close to the border with our eastern neighbours. For now, the assault group will be made up of just fifty men. Arms will flow from the armoury at Lishi. No contact will be made with garrisons at Kadah and Lapas, the nation's capital, to avoid a leak." Captain Jibo paused to light a cigarette.

"Although, ideas don't move muscles and mountains, only actions do, and a plastic should even feel secured that you will be able to efficiently handle the fifty men we plan to engage. Carefully, *passes* have been arranged for them from their various units to enable them to meet at *Ekikun* for a five-day drill and co-ordination of plans and assault details before the day. You will be given all the assistance you need to tune them to your taste. This is a war situation that has become necessary to set a new national goal, and no soldier must be deceived that all is well at present.

"From the beginning of civilization, the military had constantly intervened to right the wrongs in society. Even when there are no wars, we must create one for ourselves in order to live in peace. Peace and war are children of same parentage."

"Let me add this," Major Bellah cuts-in. "Major Boo is a signals officer. He will take charge of plans to get the radio to work for us. Code name for the country home of Major Boo is *kafejo*. It is a safe distance for operations without risking any detection. I will personally drive the two of you there in my car at the weekend for detailed final briefing on the offensive. If we..."

The interruption from the door again startled every-one. It was the barman again.

"Sir, the C.O. send one soldier say one don nak. Make I close mess. Oga, the soldier dey here sef."

10

"You mean the C.O. has ordered the mess closed?" Major Bellah barked back.

"Yes, Sir. And order is order..."!

In the military, an order from a superior officer is more profound than the rantings of a cluster of junior ones. Orders are orders and they are usually concise and often very opaque in their reels. That's what makes the military tick rather than the camouflages, steel helmets, jungle hats or jackboots very much thought about.

Thus was the footage of another full-length national dance of death successfully rehearsed at the *mess-theatre*.

order two, rule two

"...when parents mess up marriage, the children pick up the unpleasant bill..."

It was a startling assemblage of intimidating weapons for an unnecessary weird war against an established order. How such a destructive range of armour was assembled completely showed the extent of plan and the considerable secrecy that went along to prevent a leakage; ninety strong men of tested endurance, the exact number needed for a company in the regular force.

They naturally measured up to three platoons made up of infantry, armour, artillery and signals. The other corps were regarded as unnecessary for the initial putsch. It was quintessentially a destructive force whose al-chemical task in positive or negative terms may be difficult to achieve within the twelve hours set for operation *Eagle Claw*.

Major Bellah stepped out of the living room of the castle at *Ekikun* to the open courtyard. He surveyed the ninety men of armour in their games outfit. Whoever chose *Ekikun* must have taken with him to service, a good nose and a watchful eye for security details. The lake never went dry. The share size and the eco-tourism platform it represents make it a paradise for tourists but was never so in view of its remote location and distance from the capital.

"*Attention!*" Lieutenant Riwa howled as the Major stood still in his well-cut camouflage number three, the service dress. A *barretta* pistol butt reared from its holster by his hip.

"I salute every soldier here and commend you for all that you have put into the training for the past four days. Ordinarily, I just thought that you must be brought together to know one another.

"We must prevent lapses and avenues of failure. Besides, we cannot afford to lose any life to friendly fire. Since the Second World War, soldiers have learnt to fight as early as possible, to prevent a degeneration of situations. We believe that freedom is worth fighting and dying for, so that we can prevent murder, torture and slavery. What we have today is slavery in our own country and only a new military leadership can bring about the needed change.

"It may not be easy to overthrow a government that has just been democratically elected, but we must do it by sowing a seed of reformation. This seed must rust to be able to produce a new shoot and a trunk where we can harvest new fruits of development. You are to overthrow a system that is infested with lies because truth is poisoned, falsehood parades itself in a garb large enough to obscure the vicissitudes trailing it.

"By the various happenings nationwide, men and women have abandoned decency. They are like cows that soil the pasture as they graze through, only to come back seeking greener shrubs amidst a carpet of shit and politics as we understand it here is pure shit. When politics lose its charm, principally for lack of truth, everyone will pretend to be incapable of thinking right and every happening becomes an empty delight.

"What they have failed to understand is that truth is never dead. Rather, they are merely locked up in a closet. So, we have decided to bring out the truth of governance which we are equally prepared to put on display. The purity of truth is never defiled. This way, our people would know and enjoy governance.

"Operation *Eagle Claw* is a must and the D-day is now Sunday, 1st April, two days from today. You will operate in three platoons of thirty men, each headed by a Captain. The first platoon will strike at the capital, and the task is simple. You move straight to the ordinance depot where Major Momoh will be waiting. There, you will take possession of two modern *APCs* fitted with general purpose machine guns. A land-rover load of *kalashinikov* rifles with enough ammunition is already waiting there. We have the support of the Brigade Commander. Your target is the State House. Do not fire at the soldiers if they surrender willingly. Arrest the President and dispatch in a group of four each for the arrest of the defence, communications, finance and information ministers. Lieutenant Riwa will be in contact with me at the radio station where I will personally lead an assault group of six men.

"Heavens may fall at the station if the soldiers put up resistance. We will drench the entire station with cannon and rocket fire. That's our most important target, and with the station secured, the nation is secured. Communication is vital to coups.

"Platoon two, under Captain Jibo, will take charge of the northern capital of Kadah. Here, resistance is expected in view of the heavy concentration of military establishments, and the governor is expected to call in troops to counter our moves. The plan is not to fight a war of tanks and armoured vehicles, but if Kadah is difficult, you may tear limbs and drain blood.

"However, the platoon will function in sections of three MG men and seven rifle men each. In addition, two *T.55* tanks have been secured to level the entire fortress and interfering troops if issues get out of hand. Spare nothing to ensure the success of your orders."

The attention to the orders was rapt and silence was absolute. He surveyed his men for a few minutes and continued.

"Very little resistance is expected from the west and the east. Just thirty men, commanded by a Major and a Captain will carry out our operations there.

"We will have a light AIDS Department of twenty men to give support at the four locations of action. Contact has been made and loyalty secured."

Major Bellah moved away from the spot and into the formation. He suddenly stopped and his mood changed.

"Let me warn everyone seriously that this exercise must not fail. No one must fail in his duty to bring about this much needed change. Vacillation in carrying out decision on time means instant death from the man next to you. Just gun him down if you suspect that he may bring failure! Wickedness is a kind of cruelty, but you need it to succeed in this type of mission. Everyone has been briefed on how to handle his colleague to ensure maximum success. We do not plan to shed blood, but if resistance is tough, you must shoot your way to target. Understand?"

"Yeees Sir," went the wild chorus. If the clouds were light, a tear-off to heaven was imminent. That looks like the tradition in the military. Parents whose children went into the military schools often get startled at the way the little ones shout at almost everyone and everything. Peers in their streets ran errands. Old school mates listen attentively to stories of one *Sergeant Mutua* and his *dark room* gallows when the slightest mistakes are made. They talk of how they *frog jump*, *cat leap* and *back roll* during tattoos and bush camps with loud shouts of orders to which everyone must chorus 'Yees Sir'. What goes in, goes around and; even at old age, to bark and yell are effective weapons of coercion."

*   *   *

The broadcast took everyone by surprise. A guttural voice behind the microphone belching orders to the nation was designed to indicate the no-nonsense nature of another military take-over. Another giant leap backward in the national political education and a great setback to democracy in the continents' most prosperous and most densely populated black nation. If the setback to democracy was bound to anger intellectuals, its abuse formed the backdrop for organising the coup. This was noticeable in the full broadcast that followed the first announcement of the take-over.

" ...The indecent exposure to social vices by our politicians made the first coup necessary. The complete departure from the set goals to national honour, growth and advancement made this latest redemption putsch imperative. The military respects the institution of democracy considerably, and so has foiled two attempts to scuttle the democratic process. You will recall that, in handing over to the out-going civilian administration, the former head of state warned against the abandonment of the lofty ideals of democracy which is the vogue in African countries and which has, most often, resulted in military take-overs. The bane is still looming large over our lives.

"Our politicians saw democracy as a necessary tutorial for graft and robbery. Morality became an irritant to many office holders. National conscience no longer worth any value as we all acted like bottle-throwing hoodlums. Within five years, our economy nose-dived into a recession that now requires a tough action to rescue. Social services have been paralysed with our schools becoming mere tout resorts and centres of similar vices. The hospitals have become mere consulting centres and slaughterhouses.

"Our democracy allowed everything except proper management of our national life and our politicians had a bit of everything except taste, wit and intelligence. They pride themselves in their stubborn refusal to admit error even after having made the most monumental of miscalculations about the national economy and vital foreign policies. They exposed us indecently to conspicuous consumption that ruined our economy and made in us, a people living more out of desperation than inspiration. Our monarchs, who could have called them to order merely proliferate titles and adulate recipients on occasions of conferment. The royal fathers themselves have become more decadent and less capable of ruling and counseling their subjects.

"Consequently, the members of the armed forces again decided to put a stop to this national drift. No point whispering into a hurricane anymore. We can no longer fold our arms and watch things rot away and, with it, the future of our children.

"All politicians, with their rosy cheeks and heft as if their milk and meal were over-laden with estrogen and carcinogen are to report immediately to the nearest police posts or any military formation. Anyone flouting this order without reasonable clarification will be ruthlessly dealt with. Such clarification, if feigned, will equally *clarify* such a person out of existence! This new regime will not tolerate any act of indiscipline. Law and order will be strictly maintained, and security agencies have been instructed to deal decisively with anyone attempting to seize the situation in the country to cause confusion.

"We will not respect any hierarchy or fame that is intended for use to undermine the success of this regime. Orders will be given, and such orders must be maintained and obeyed. Our orders remain our orders..."

Orders were actually orders, and they came out in large numbers and rapid succession, the arresting quality and common feature being their artlessness and the assortment of legal terminologies rendered in military ruthlessness.

The putschists were not too well known. Only their well-starched camouflage uniforms recreated a typical *Green Beret* scene on television in the evening news. It was a low-band recording and the reality and greenness were too exact.

"I know that Major Bellah! I know him very well." The discussion stirred at the University Guest House as two lecturers listened to the evening news on television.

"He was a lieutenant during the civil war. He fought in the northern command and was the *recce* man for the 109 Brigade that captured the military capital of the rebel soldiers. In fact, stories had it that a bullet whistled across his jaw, ripping off some teeth and considerable gum. But for surgery and denture, you could mistake him for a cleft lip and palate patient. Even with that, they said he was the longest serving officer in the war. He started with them, and ended with them. If you can ..."

"You must be of the same parentage! You know too much to be too distant from these mad guys who should be rounded-up, executed and buried in shallow graves!" Dr. Amba Zuma, a senior lecturer in political science exploded in annoyance at the unfolding events in the last seven hours.

"What did they do wrong, Dr. Zuma?"

"So many things, Mr. Rimiba. So many things that a lecturer in accountancy such as you, may not understand. What I am seeing on the screen is a pure assemblage of idiots who are again determined to take the nation off-course and thereafter announce a national search for unity. Like an unsuccessful charge-and-bail lawyer, hawking sedition and libel, they will only dispense graft, poverty, squalor, retrenchment and consequently introduce a new wave of armed robbery to our young ones. You know that when parents mess up marriage, it is the children who pick up the unpleasant bill. Very soon, our young ones will pick up the rough and tough life of the military. I am sure that we are too likely to move from plenty to want and from there to absolute lack! Mark those words; *absolute lack! Absolute lack!* That's it!"

Dr. Zuma was always electrifying in his speeches. The news soon ended and the analysis was rife in many homes, just as in the University Guesthouse.

"My friend, an armed uprising against the State is an act of treason, and the penalty is death! These boys should be executed. Why in this country must our military boys always stage coups each time one man goes gaga? Why? It is like going out to arrest the village blacksmith each time that a man commits murder with a machet. No use! You read meanings to mistakes only when you have an ulterior motive. Our boys had always nursed motives of becoming presidents, ministers, administrators and all that kind of rot. It is uncharitable to mistrust the state and her functionaries without credible reason. We were not complaining about our functionaries, and so, we had no reason for the coup. No experiment is a complete failure; it will serve as a good or bad example for a valuable lesson, especially when it is politics. These boys are mad. In fact, these bullies, these hot heads and sly guys are what they must be; mad! And...."

"You lavish too much pity on these politicians while you forget the misery they put us into," Mr. Rimiba cuts-in.

"We had democracy all right, but we never smelt *meritocracy*. I don't think that the overthrown civilian administration had any decorum. It merely rattled in opportunities and was constantly scared of the virtues of merit. If we must cast out the demon in us, we must apply the right incantation and discourage *theftocracy*.

"Getting things done is not the same as getting them done well. The politicians just did not do things well. They needed this *tonic* and I see militarism as the best of the worst," Mr. Rimiba submitted.

"And this *tonic* must necessarily be to use the money of the state to buy *FN* riffles to commit regicide and thereafter organise support rallies nationwide...?" Dr. Zuma queried.

"But you saw the ostentation that ran riot in our national life. You saw how everyone sought refuge in extravagant illusions. You know what is happening in this apex university, about millions being drained into private pockets with probe panels merely barking and not being able to bite. You also..."

"Mr. Accountant, the worst politician is still better than the best soldier. He disagrees without being dis-agreeable. A soldier disagrees and settles his score with bullets as if bullets were national analgesics. Look, if temper could improve the longer we kept it, then, our democracy will improve the longer we are allowed to run it. This is not our salvation. Maybe we must apply the eastern approach: advertise for someone to takeover the country and rule it for five years, operating like the general manager of a company. If he fails to turn the country around for good, execute him. If he succeeds, give him, Grand Commander medal."

"That's right, Doc. But you are a political scientist and you can do better than the lampooning of these action boys in khaki while defending politicians that are always running a race behind schedule. I will advise that you organise a national news conference and in your address, invite the British and beg Her Majesty that: *sorry o, we made mistake o! Radicals like me have discovered that my country was not ripe for self-rule and that there are no animals with enough wisdom to occupy the Government House. Please come back and govern us, Your Majesty, for the next 100 years.'* Of course, you know what you will make of your qualification and that national lease-hold?"

"What? But I would have told the truth. The plastic truth that cannot be changed."

"No! You would have made a big fool of your education..."

"No...! You are the greater fool, Mr. Accountant. People of your type who believe that military intervention is the solution to every political mistake are this country's version of Simon Newcomb: that astronomer who once declared that airplane as a flying machine was utterly impossible. After many trials and errors, including the death of entire families sometimes, man is today going safely by air in various versions of the airplane. You are making the same mistake with democracy in this country. Our politicians are good. Just give them the chance to learn on the job."

"All I know is that these boys aren't fools. No fool leads a revolt. Only wise men do."

"Oh, yes, and their wisdom will be coming in salvoes of orders, commands, pronouncements and decrees. In fact, we have begun a new season, a new order in chaos and our collective consciousness about what politics should mean has again been aborted, but the intellectual..." The waiter suddenly interrupted Dr. Zuma.

"*Oga Sir, another Head of State don come. Turn television to National Station, the man dey talk there. He dey radio sef*".

The interruption stopped the debate involuntarily and by reflex, the television knob had flicked the set to the national channel to behold the new Head of State, General Ramos Baguludu, a tall fair-complexioned and handsome man. He effortlessly read his speech from a prepared script in a particularly piquant fashion.

"...The Revolutionary State Council (*RSC*) made up of officers from the service forces, after meeting few hours back, has appointed me, General Ramos Baguludu, as the new Head of State and Supreme Commander of the Armed Forces.

"As the first step towards sanitizing the system, all detained politicians will be subjected to trial. Military tribunals are hereby set up with immediate effect to try them. All diplomatic passports have been cancelled and any movement outside our borders, now opened for operations between 8 a.m. and 6 p.m., must be cleared at the National Security Headquarters.

"All international conferences and seminars for all grades of officers in the service have been cancelled. Henceforth, importation of all types of printing papers into this country is banned. This administration has discovered that too many newspapers contributed to the crazy rivalry between our politicians. It is an unnecessary waste of our scarce resources. This administration will oversee the press and any newspaper house overstepping its bounds will be closed down.

"The civil service will be thoroughly sanitized from the decadence brought upon it by politics. The civil servants have now discovered that any civilian administration is an equivalent of a nuclear explosion, especially at election periods during which we spend too much and achieve too little. It is usually a new order in chaos. Any civil servant finding it difficult to cope with our pace will be retired. In line with this innovation, all redundant officials now littering the ministries as a result of unguided and selfish recruitment policies are hereby relieved of their posts. Such category of officers includes those recruited to grade levels 04-09 within the last six months of the sacked administration.

"We know what is going on in the service. It is common knowledge that our own service is the most corrupt in Africa where both junior and senior officers play the role of surrogate politicians to loot the treasury. A study by a non-governmental body recently revealed that outside of government, civil servants are the most eligible buyers of new cars when contractors make do with second hand or fairly used ones. Today, they are the richest class in the country.

"The high-scale insincerity must stop. In fact, this administration will trim the ministries. We will stop government money from going into individual pockets. No country progresses when public funds are stolen to make individuals richer than the government they serve.

"The size of the nation's mission abroad is hereby reduced in view of the ostentation that has drained our country's foreign reserves. Our university system is no longer what it was designed to be. Lecturers are daily making revolutionaries out of our young ones. The universities now function as ideological training centres that are considerably anti-establishment. This administration will not tolerate politician-lecturers any longer. Security agencies have been alerted to discover and bring to book such lecturers. Moreover..." And the television suddenly went dead with a violent touch from Dr. Zuma who jumped from his seat in a manner more likely to suggest that he was prepared to settle his scores with the military, matching the pen with the gun.

"Enough is enough! This is just like listening to passages from *The Seven Masterpieces of Gothic Horror*. I hate seeing that man in the lotus position he assumed behind the multitude of microphones and klieg light. I must go."

"You gave me a rude shock. Dr. Zuma" Mr. Rimiba finally found words in his askance position symbolizing considerable disappointment at the action of Dr. Zuma.

"If you must go, must we shut our eyes and minds to happenings around us? You are what you are because of longing and lager. The longing to be something you actually do not know and the lager that has beaded your brows with the sweat of envy."

"Why? Can't you distinguish between signs of excitement, terror and intoxication? Intoxication is already falling in torrents in just a few hours in office...

"If there is anyone to be tried and summarily executed, you are the one. You have committed high treason. You have allowed emotion, laden with unuseful 'isms,' to overshadow your intelligence such that you now find it difficult to respect the head of state. You must watch out! This cloud of rubbish in your head will lead you into detention." Mr. Rimiba's warning appeared to be a timely one for a one-man riot squad against state authority. Little did he know that the unfolding events were mere scoutmasters of greater surprises for which the new military junta would be famous.

Maybe it is a spell that the military in Africa must always produce oppressors. Giant men of armour who reach to the skies and bend only to pick the golden morsels, must be left to select oppressors who dance from everywhere to a stage of steel. They are made daily from the ivory towers, the one-room business centres of their cousins, the motor-parks and other sectors of non-relevance. The game is simple: to allow the rich they have created to oppress the poor to an extent that the poor ones lose focus and quarrel among themselves.

order three, rule three

"...and they poisoned politics from source by camping together for regicide."

"Look here, everyone of you! Open your ears well!"

"Yes Sir!"

"O.K! Soldiers without orders are no soldiers. I give orders... You obey my orders... O.K.?"

"Yes Sir!"

"I be RSM for this barrack. Fall in at six, you must fall-in at six. Now see that soldier. He just dey come ten minutes past six. Your wife no allow you wake up eh? You no say army no owe you anything more than death gratuity and one small cofin as NCO if you die on top of woman?

"No, Sir!" the answer came from Corporal John with whom he was trading gazes in his stone dead posture.

"Wetin happen then? I say wetin happen? You dey play with guardroom, now, now!" When *RSMSs* roar orders and statements, they are merely terrifying the boys to blind obedience to military discipline.

"I am sorry, Sir! I was on guard last night. I have just closed because my relief didn't come quick. The Colonel G.S quarter was my duty post, and I was supposed to be off duty before you suddenly ordered me out for this special parade, Sir."

"*Last warning, you hear? Next time if you no fall in at 6 a.m., you fall out of the Army forever! You hear me so? Excuse no go bring sympathy again O. Oya, fall for line, you go sign for rifle later.*" RSM Bala barked out as he properly positioned himself near the podium to address the section of ten men in full battle gear.

"*Yes, oga go come talk to you now. My own na to get you here. I no know how to talk at all. Na oga go come talk, my own na order and I don use order carry you for line. No be so?*"

"*Na so, Sir!*" they chorused.

"No, Sir! You are dead quiet sir," Corporal John who was just permitted to fall on line chipped in.

"*Shuuut-up! Who ask you to talk?*" the RSM barked out.

"I am only obeying question order, Sir! Sorry, sir for..."

"*Shuuun! Oga don come!*" the RSM put everyone firmly on his legs as the young lieutenant mounted the dais to have few words with the men. He was brisk in his rendition.

"Good morning. You have been specially selected for the State House swearing-in ceremony this morning. You will also form the nucleus of the Special Protection Group (*SPG)* for the President as from today. The President will swear-in all military governors and ministers at just one ceremony and everything will be done with military dispatch. Your order is simple. Nothing, absolutely nothing, must be allowed to disturb the ceremony." He paused a while as if he was assessing the column of tanks and assault guns milling around the parade ground.

"You are to cordon off the entire state house annex. Choose your points of location for a proper view on rooftops and other vantage areas. Five of you will ensure that no guns are brought into the council chambers. *Aide-de-camps* of officers to be sworn-in are to drop their weapons or stay outside. Only the President goes in with his weapon. Understand?"

"Yes, Sir!"

"Carefully selected *APC's* and *Scout Cars* were rolled to location few hours back and with your military training, you will easily identify the *CCD* crew by their red mufflers. You will move to location in the ferret Jeeps provided here and tanks will be ready to move to location, just in case.

"The Containment, Camouflage and Deception, (*CCD*) crew, will bring in the President and shut the door against everyone when the General has taken his seat. You must look like a bunch of hungry gorillas building a security atmosphere that will be completely impenetrable and repelling. No convulsions at all. If there is any lapse, don't come back to depot."

*   *   *

Two appointments and two orders were most startling as the head of state, adopting the title of a President, conferred authority on aides at the council chambers. Standing tallest behind the massive oak table taking the oath of allegiance before General Baguludu was thirty five-year-old Lieutenant Colonel Yom Yizor, whose youthfulness, a factor which gave out his age, brought him more attention amongst the ten other military governors. He did not mortgage any trait of his vitality when he took the oath as if he was reciting the beatitudes in his local church. The climax came as the master of ceremony announced what the audience, especially the press, least expected: Dr. Amba Zuma, as Minister for Information. He stepped out in his French suit, grim-faced in his usual revolutionary posture. He took his oath and accepted the handshake from the President with both hands, followed by a loud ovation that recharged the *CCD* team who promptly issue out warnings against celebrations. The vogue is to jostle for position with any government in power and celebrate the selection in all manners of clothing colours and with all kinds of drinks.

General Baguludu's short but loaded speech that contained some startling orders, was simply titled *"Camp Out With Me."*

"You have discovered that there is nothing to be joyful about in our years of political freedom without wisdom. This administration is out to correct that inverted approach to development. No doubt, any democratic government must run on opinions. That's why all its achievements must equally rest on the human and material development of the country.

"But this administration will not arrogate a return to any unnecessary democratic atmosphere that will delay processes and stall growth as earlier announced in my first broadcast. However, this administration will always communicate with the good people of this nation. Whether such communications are seen as complicated ideas, hard choices, lack of alternatives or not too pleasant news, will not be the issue. The issue will be that we are moving ahead to achieve results. This administration will not allow any rising tide to rock our boat. You are called to do business of redemption with me and that's exactly what you must do. You either get going or get out. In developed countries, democracies are today transforming into social insurance states. Here, we are still not aware of what a state must be. I did not choose you by accident or lassitude, but after serious considerations of your credentials. And, after today, you must continue to move mountains in the states and ministries for which you are accounting officers.

"To ensure that you stay on course to do the business of government you have been appointed to do, the following will be your working orders:

No governor shall be permitted to use sirens in the conduct of government business. You are on military assignment, and all force of military discipline will be brought upon misbehaving governors. You will not be addressed as 'Your Excellencies'. See yourselves as part of the larger state community. No security vote shall be spent beyond 'x' volume, and 'x' volume is the level already approved by me and to be communicated to you by the Accountant-General of the Federation after this ceremony.

"You will not appoint more than six commissioners to help you in the conduct of government business, and those appointed must not live in government quarters. As military officers on military appointments, you can equally be removed anytime you fall short of the mandate of your offices. You must not embark on new projects for now. Concentrate on the completion of the on-going ones. Any report of departure from these guidelines means automatic military action against any state governor.

"Remember that we are soldiers and not civilians. We are tightly knitted, unlike them who are always in flowing gowns that get stuck into all kinds of unpleasant hindrances. This administration is in office to sweep clean, and we will do this thoroughly. To this end, a three-member military tribunal, headed by Brigadier-General Jerry Mawoju, has been constituted and sworn-in this morning to try all detained politicians. I can assure you that those rosy cheeks will become shrunk again and the stolen nation's resources recovered. The tribunal is to conclude the trials in three months..."

*   *   *

Banner headlines dominated the papers the next day. The appointment of Dr. Zuma and the lurid account of his swearing-in and his refusal to grant press interview made the news.

"I fear for Dr. Zuma," the discussion picked up at the foyer of the University Library, between his faculty dean and the chief librarian.

"You just can't wind and unwind him. He is not a nuts-and-bolts man who will zoom in and out as dictated by part-one orders from the State House at Lilipond Barracks."

"Let us wait and see, Sir," the chief librarian calmed issues.

"No, there is no point waiting to see anything. The President has thrown a jewel at a lion. General Baguludu has put radicalism on the line since day one and I can tell you exactly when Dr. Zuma will zoom out of government. Consider his line of antagonism with previous governments and the President's statements that he was going to tamper with the press. Radical university lecturers are to be trailed, monitored and fished out for punishment. Military tribunals have been set up to try detained politicians and the Bar Association has been sternly advised to steer clear."

"Damn! Damn," the librarian retorted and disappeared into his office, leaving the dean with the crowding students now getting impressed with his tirade.

"*Oga*, we may be surprised... Dr. Zuma will bleach his conscience clean within the next few weeks," one of the students put in a few words.

"That's true, Sir! And it's already happening. Look at it, the man didn't grant press interview. This is the same man who granted interviews to any newspaper that cared to ask for one. In fact, a sweep-car wailed into campus this morning leading other trucks to cart off his property and family against the pronouncement on the usage of siren.

"He is no longer with us. To leave his position and accept a portfolio under an undemocratic government is scandalous. His cupboard will soon be full of skeletons."

"That's right Fella," the dean gloated, obviously impressed.

"Zuma is always angry with any system. He wants to serve a government in whose concept and foundation he had no part. He will come back angry.

"It will now be a silly session at the staff club and debates will be low-ebbed. I pray he gets angry quick and gets out fast. He's a chattering class and he can't endure being stored like a bullet in an armoury."

*   *   *

The debate was equally lengthy at the officers' mess at *Oke-Amun Barracks*. It was a full house of army officers coming out to the mess for the first time after the coup. Events have now taken enough shape to enable officers talk openly and in line with the swinging of the pendulum.

"*Your wife don open wardrobe and you don commot? Na so so yabis and sakara now, eh?*" Major Sauda pulled one on a fellow major.

"*Sharrap! You think say I be you wey go run go sick leave when you just hear martial music? Me, Major Joseph, I don sign for this army work. You hear? I dey committed to any coup any day.*"

34

"Tell the truth. You hid in your wife's wardrobe?" Major Dauda insisted.

"Ask about me from my commander. Where I pitch my camp, I stay there. I don't know impossibilities. As an army engineer, I led a demolition company during the war, detecting and breaching mines for our troops to move in and fight. Coup come, *I dey. The thing fail, I dey.* Even if it is mutiny, my God, it is fight to finish!"

"O.K, why didn't you join them to organize this one?"

"You nko? Why you no join them. Now, you commot come dey talk nonsense. Soja get mouth when you never put handcuff for dem hand sha."

"Look, Major, *na wah o!* I served at the Barima Cantonment and our commander ordered the general manager of the state radio to create airtime to support late Major Akpan's coup. There I learnt my lesson. You are aware that the coup failed. *Our oga and the man were arrested, tried and executed and the general manager never see gun before o! Since that day, if I hear coup for radio, nah for radio I go hear the final before I talk to anybody!"* the Major came out frankly.

"Can you imagine what even happened?" Major Dauda also opened up with all seriousness. "You see that boy that was with me at the 302 Regiment, Lieutenant Riwa, that daring boy who came from the Riverside Ordinance Depot?"

"Oh yes, that boy who won the commander's sword for the best student in pistol firing and..."

"That's right. Riwa was the leader of the hit squad that stormed the presidential lodge and arrested the

35

President. He is now the commander of the *SPG*. By their orders, they will be the best protection and assault group ever in existence in this country. It is a team of 200 men made up of soldiers, sailors and airmen with proven competence in karate and knife fighting, scuba diving, stunt diving and weapons handling from pistol to sniper rifle. With them, this military president will become an institution. No coup will remove him, Allah!

"The *Special Protection Group* has been trained not to know what is impossible. They will use heart and brain, muscle and spirit to ensure protection for the president and, of course, this regime. Let me warn again that if any soldier thinks that he can overthrow that man, he is joking and playing with court martial. He will step out only when he wants to step out and he may even re-emerge later in mufti."

"Major, *the man get brain o*! Since he led the *'Belting Operation'* to quell the bloody riot at Zimbaba, I have learnt to fear him. Don't be deceived by that funny window frame between his canine. The man will just do anything, no matter what the people say. *I fear o*. By the time he finishes with this country, we won't know who ruled us again."

"I agree with you. With the little I know of him, the man can order you to do anything, even if it is inimical to your existence. By the time you finish, he will ask you if the initiative of execution was not taken by you. *Haba*! The man is too theatrical. He can order that the quarter guard in his barracks be disbanded. If, later in the day, he drove to that point and finds no guards to pay him compliments, he will order the *RSM* arrested for dereliction of duty. *Nah wah for the man*! The man is pure theatre, I maintain "

"You think he will cannibalize the army?" Major Dauda became charged.

"Of course. Don't talk about that again. Military leadership in Africa without the cannibalism of the army is like a circle without an ark, a geometric invalid. He is now a politician, and you know that conspiracy is the charm of politics. He will conspire with the few officers with him and cannibalize the army, principally to make any coup impossible. But no sensible soldier will attempt a coup in this country when he is in power. You know that he is a master planner. He can plan a coup even against his wife."

"Ah! I am only sorry for those politicians who allowed a man with a monstrous penis, obtained through careful plastic surgery, to have a carnal knowledge of his wife, thereby infesting her with a disease. They are applauding now at the immoral act and gloating that the disease is curable at little cost. Very soon, the woman will start going from doctor to doctor in search of a cure. By the time orders continue to roll over orders, offering them political settlement fabrics of dissimilar materials, they will come to their senses and lavish pity on themselves."

*   *   *

The *Oke-Amun Barracks* officers' mess became an unsuccessful military arena for retailing slander against the President for many nights until it eventually became the camping ground and tribunal venue for prosecuted politicians. The gossips ceased. For months, the trials went on and life at the mess became drab and silly. The terms of imprisonment startled the officers.

Various terms were handed down. The case of the former Minister for Health, Chief Asom Tatalo was interesting. His trial on a rip-off of almost one hundred million naira built into a three hundred-million naira contract for the supply of drugs to some teaching hospitals had dragged on for weeks. At the close of sitting on one of the days, he asked the tribunal chairman, Brigadier General John Odu, a favour.

"I am not complaining about my trial, Sir. In fact, I can't complain. But I request that you move me out of this mess. I can't reconcile the entire issue. In one moment, my room is flooded with assorted beer, even without my request. The next moment, I take few steps to face a stern-looking military panel and cross-examiners, forcing hard facts down my throat.

"I think I need to see the outside world a bit, relax my mood and tension by walking or being driven a distance before the next phase of my predicament. I am a diabetic's patient and you flood my room daily with lager but refused me access to my drugs. You will soon kill me. I am losing weight too rapidly."

Brigadier Odu looked straight into his eyes and gave him more hellish thoughts. "My friend, the authority has decided to put you here and equally try you here.

There is no complaint at all. You didn't think of this devastating monotony of life when you inflated a contract because you wanted to build a brewery. A minister of health for that matter! I think you should have even gone into tobacco trade. We will soon transfer you to a farther place. In fact, you people are disturbing our officers. They are no longer coming to the mess."

The fourth day, his case was decided. He was sentenced to seventy-five years imprisonment on four counts at his over ripe age of sixty-two. The least for anyone was forty years, and quite a handful went to prison for life. Tribunal sentences were fun.

Dr. Zuma was to come out as the Minister for Information to defend the sentences. He did that on the occasion of the swearing-in of the new director for external information monitoring in his ministry.

The reporter of the *National Newsreel* got him to talk to the press for the first time.

"Do you think the tribunal was thorough, given the time frame permitted by the President, Sir?"

"Well, I do not think the trial was rushed. The members performed within reasonable pace, considering their timing and the number of accused persons."

"How many were tried, or are still being tried, Sir?"

"You see, the government cannot be exact. We keep on picking up people every day as the result of investigation dictates. This government, you must know, is attempting to be a thorough and corrective regime. The avalanche of work being done underground, to sanitize the entire system and national fabric, is much and great care must be taken to ensure that good intentions are not allowed to derail. We have seen governments which started well and ended badly. We do not want a government of that nature."

"But the sentences, Sir. Some people felt they are bogus, especially the Minister of State for finance who was sentenced to one hundred and eighty-seven years imprisonment."

"No sentence passed up to now has been outrageous or bogus. It was proved that he stole money and he was penalised. This government has started a system of mass mobilisation against unit demobilisers considered inimical to our national existence. We must socially re-orientate our people against graft. We must re-direct their ethics toward more rewarding goals. This is the beginning and we must relentlessly pursue the worthy directives of this administration. These unit demobilisers are at work in every arm of government and facet of the society. For a good job to be done, the military is commencing by purging itself.

"We have for long majored in the minor and prided ourselves in pedantic arrogance without a commitment to any clear-cut national goal. Spain had her own Franco, China her own Mao, Germany her own Hitler, we now have our own Baguludu. Before the push to the El Dorado by our heartless brothers and sisters becomes a shove; before corruption is tattooed into every heart, surgical operations like these are necessary. Our past is irritating and, if we control the present, we will be able to master the future of our people and nation. Our approach in correcting these irregularities is based on the premise that there are no saints without a past as there are no sinners without a future. This country has a past. We are the present and, maybe, you are the future! Maybe..."

"This assignment may be too demanding, Sir?"

"Yes, we know this and as we have declared to the people, we will tamper with the press and spy on the people, and any bone overladden with too much flesh, we will gladly graft. We need more of the noble than the nibble men we parade now, and you will agree with me that the meal times are gone."

They are gone actually but not from every table. They merely shifted to another table where *ADCs*, batmen and security personnel kept vigil over them for their bosses.

order four, rule four

"...and they always rush to make the list, but they never made it."

"Dem plenty here, Sir
And better one dey,
Correct price,
Double sow!
Pure cotton!
Original TKB!
Fifty, fifty naira each.
Make I bring am, oga?"

"Get out and don't block my view. In actual fact, you are tampering with my side mirror!"

"Sorry, Sir. This is original tie!
Original TKB. Nothing like it for dis country.
Try am, you go come back buy more!
How many I go bring?"

"My God! Leave me alone. I don't want any tie! And don't tamper with my side mirror!" Taylor Cruz shouted indignantly to rid himself of the nuisance of the hawker and his sweet dribblings, the marketing strategy that is becoming a growing feature of the traffic congestion at the nation's capital.

Traffic was at a complete standstill and business transaction was at the peak. Boys hawking items, from cutlery to jewellery, radio and automobile parts, litter the two-kilometre fly-over from the Government Secretariat to the central bus stop on the mainland. What a beautiful place it used to be. Highly noted for her cool breeze and highbrow shopping malls that gracefully added to its reputation as the old marine area. The beauty is now gone and the entire marine-line littered with makeshift shops, barbing salons and hawking stands resulting from a liberalized economy booming with second-hand materials.

"Oga, try one now."

"Oh my God! I said I don't want your T.K....what?"

"T.K.B., Sir!" he helped to complete the acronym with laughter.

"What is *TKB* by the way?"

"Ah oga, you never hear TKB? Big man like you? No be you dash us? Oga genara come power and see say poor man dey suffer when those long throat politicians dey enjoy. He come say make border open to bring different, different goods inside. Come see now, everything don arrive and we go dey enjoy. We come give am name: Tokunboh or TKB for short.

This genara like poor man o!

How many I go bring, Sir?

Na double sow

Correct material

No ironing

Fairly use

Already dry clean!"

"Is that so?"

"*Yes, Sir! You must to adjust o. Before traffic move, which one you prefer. Complete red or blue. Spotted one dey sef.*"

"Adjust to what?"

"*Oga, no bi una dey read budget? You come dey ask for adjustment from we common people for on top bridge? No be you dey budget? Wetin common people know? We get anything to budget as you dey see us so? Oga, adjust na to adjust ourselves and our pocket properly so that di thing we dey buy for ten naira, we go dey buy for two naira from now on. Chineke bless this genara o! But you surprise me oga! No be secretariat you dey come? If you no hear am for secretariat, you know see newspaper and people wey dey hold solidarity rally for government every where?*"

He stood back and looked straight into his eyes from the side of the Nissan trooper car as his reluctant customer inched off in the crawling traffic without concentration.

"*Oga! Look front! You don...*"

Plast! Ghast! Ghasses! And it was done.

The man had smashed the complete rear lights of the mercedes benz car ahead.

"What a hell! This would have been avoided," he cried out his thoughts loudly as they flashed, "but for this devil that disturbed my concentration!"

In that twinkle, the hawking boys had gathered and hooting from restless drivers was mounting from behind but no trace of the real culprit; he had vanished.

"Sorry, please. I am very sorry, and we can settle this between ourselves without the police. Actually, I was distracted," he accepted blame apologetically as the all gray-haired man accosted him to assess the damage and the delay he was likely to cause. That was Lapas, a city where everyone rushed to nowhere.

"No problems. Just hand over your papers and you pick them as soon as you settle me. I am Colonel Sanni Buka of the Military Police Unit. Hand the papers over to my orderly, quickly. Ten o'clock tomorrow at the *Kayede Barracks*, all right? Come with your mechanic!" And he was off.

The sweat was much on Mr Cruz as he carefully unbuttoned his silk shirt to reveal the hairs on his scrawny chest with pronounced nipples that ordinarily made a mountain out of a molehill. He was far away in thought and unconscious of the mournful glees around him

"Oga, you dey lucky self, the man na gentle man soldier. But no go dem barrack o! Go repair the car for workshop. The thing go dey too costly for barrack. My brother dey sell original Benz spare part under the bridge. Rear light no cost. Efen sef, fairly use TKB dey! Make I run go bring am?"

"Shuuut-uup! What a hell? One of you caused this accident with your *TKB* this, *TKB* that. Now see...."

"Oga, we dey different, different o. For me, I don't force people to buy market. If na me dey sell for you, you no go get this kin accident. Na man must wack business the other boy won do. That one no good! Oga, make I go bring am? Sometime self you fit buy fairly-use TKB. That one no cost like original TKB. That one sef different from the real original. As money no dey town now, we fit put the fairly

*use TKB inside real original packet. Oga soldier no go
know because we for don cello-tape am well, well! Na
apriko we dey call that kind method."*

"God Almighty! I must get out of this mess!" he was
thinking aloud again as he regained the awareness
needed to catch up with the army officer going away
with his vehicle papers.

We had growth, a growth in the opposite direction
that bears no correlation between a population of over
a hundred million and her gross domestic product. The
monies get to the hands but they are tied to nothing
before they fly away; *ego nefu efu, ego nefu efu,* was a
common tribal cliché. We had growth and confusion
took a great leap forward. Boys who tried to look like
men confuse the roads with weird driving styles at day.
And at night, they equally drive residents in remote
streets to madness and fright, unleashing terror and
destruction. They cart off anything, from money to
trinkets, and fancifully display the trinkets round their
thin necks on bare bodies the next day. The pendants
dangle between their shrinking nipples. It was our
growth pattern. And the girls, the often too tender girls
willing to look like women, fancy such ways. They are
nothing but babies. Babies whose lower lips will quiver
and their sunken eyes rain ceaseless water at a mere
yell. From their underwears to their tops, it was a
season of *Tokunbos,* representing growth in illusion and
falsehood. The younger generation that must be taught
the value of honesty, virtue and hard work were told
to strive to 'make it' at all costs. Their tutor parents

the lesson of history that wealth is not synonymous with happiness and contentment.

The parents, most of them with infant profiles, are also quick to rain curses on a nation whose future they have plundered with their greed. *God bless America... Long live the King* are daily prayers in countries we emulate, but when a little push is applied to keep order, our reaction is: *This country can never know peace shah!* Our marked propensity in vanity is without parallel and because we so much adore the false gods of power; money and wealth, our inadequacies increased daily. The consciousness of a vain world has consumed us and we have consequently strayed away from the path of honour. We built a city of beauty and destroyed everything therein by our restlessness and passion for indecency.

*   *   *

Such was the nature of the capital city that a thorough mess was created of every part. All manner of imports, all manner of junks and all nature of trade prospered, even at the shoulder and sidewalks of city expressways. Lapas was clearly becoming a city of congestion and the Government was becoming startled about the consequences of its growing orders to bring about sanity. Well, since orders must be orders and you constantly need a new set of them to bring in sanity; orders, even when they arouse displeasure, anger or irritation, must be issued. In Lapas, only the insane can deal with the insane. Sanity seldom works. The City Environmental Committee, headed by Major Lash Meno, was to do the job of restoring social and environmental sanity. This proved a very difficult park. Lapas was daily becoming a city of numerous lapses by a grossly disobedient population. The committee saw hell!

"Your Excellency, the boys are merely taking full advantage of our deregulation," the economic planning minister opined when the issue came up for discussion at the council meeting. It was the only agenda on the council paper accompanied by a booklet of newspaper cuttings on the fast deteriorating state of the capital. Lapas was no doubt the dirtiest capital city in the whole country. Hawkers were daily making the city an irritable junkyard. The pace of their own approach to modernity was daily creating unnecessary stress and horrifying restlessness and there was need to turn the dwellers clock back to a time long before the *Y2K* problems began.

"Yes, I know them. They are very astute business-men, but we may deregulate ourselves out of comfort if care is not taken. The anticipated gain of deregulation is firstly, to clear the mess of nonchalance," General Baguludu chipped in before sipping from his glass of processed water, a recent vogue in Lapas with countless packs daily emerging from kitchenettes and bathrooms which serve as production centres. They display their strength as *poor water* rather than pure water. Hawking is mostly on the bridges, highways and motor-parks.

"The works minister has complained that our network of city bridges may not last their life span. He told the city dwellers as constantly as the opportunity presents itself that when the traffic flows, not much weight is recorded on the bridges, but a standstill of many hours weakens the structure and collapse is imminent. This could be tragic. But city people, it appears, are used to tragic situations. The traffic barriers against heavy duty trucks at the foot of the bridges are removed and twisted the next day they are installed.

"The minister has also reported that six of the geesink-sweepers bought recently to keep the city clean have broken down completely. You will agree with me that Major Lash Meno has been trying. In fact, I have invited him here to address this council on what to do about the deteriorating situation in the capital city. Let him talk! Major, common talk to us."

The situation must actually be grave, such that a non-council member and a junior officer would move a memo during a council meeting. This duty is normally for council members only.

Major Meno, an inner city boy whose burly stature and deafening orders in major streets could melt gun barrels, stood up from a lone seat close to the entrance of the council chambers. He was in full battle gear. His number one camouflage was starched to razor edge precision with the trouser tucked into an oil resistant pair of jungle boots laced knee high.

Carrying his helmet on one hand and a paper on the other, he moved from his seat to the dais facing the president in a twinkle, like a genet.

"Major, you are in war mood!" General Baguludu teased.

"Yes, Sir. But a no-win war, Sir. My thundering barrages of verbal and drill artillery have not, and are not capable of winning us the war. This society, Sir, is fast decaying. All manner of decency, decorum and cleanliness have gone with the winds. Our people have incredibly locked themselves inside the unpleasant intricacies of high pressure living.

"Sir, my assignment is to keep this city clean and bring pride to our government and people. But as a soldier, we prepare comprehensive reports about our bush exercises. I thus went outside my mandate to advise on a very important issue of location as reflected by the title of my paper which is *'Bye-bye Lapas.'* "

"I hope you have not thrown away your commission?"

"God forbid, my General. No soldier throws away his commission easily. So, I am still keeping mine, but with what I have seen and experienced within the past months, Sir, this city and her inhabitants possess a devilish cult gift of remaining absolutely still and never shifting in habits and social ways that are in conformity with the civilised society. No idea is workable in Lapas. No legislation is respected. No environment is seen more than a dump, a junkyard or a *pooh-pooh* shade. We have run out of steam. This city is highly inattentive and the chattering classes are too irredeemable from destructive tendencies. The sense of indecency is soaring daily.

"Your Excellency, we have disbursed over fifty million naira of the current budget on sanitation campaigns, and my frequency of news conferences with convulsive news outflow, hitherto unparalleled by any ministerial department, has not achieved anything. It appears that there is a conspiracy by these city rats to just say *no* to everything.

"The inglorious thing is that every individual, group and corporate body is in the business of spoiling Lapas. Imagine Sir, that advert companies involved in image making have turned out to be the greatest agents for image destruction. At the high class *Ikorobi* Boulevard, they tear off and re-paste posters on bill boards daily and this is done as rapidly as my boys pack them. One would think that in advert companies, the staff would be above average in their decency and pack the mess for central disposal. But no! Compared with the posters that they paste, they are far less decent.

"We had once reached an agreement to pull down all kind of boards along the streets, and approval to re-erect will be granted strictly and only on local government recommendations. But just as we were contemplating this, the plan leaked and the innocuous agencies were already negotiating with landlords to use their rooftops as advert spaces.

"Later, my committee discarded the language of morality in dealing with these people. We allowed instant temperament to dictate our handling of the abusive use of our city. But even with that, it was serious labour before achieving anything." Major Meno paused to wipe beads of sweat making their way through his forehead in the fully air-conditioned council chamber.

"Your Excellency, I have travelled very extensively for training courses in my ten years of service. I have travelled, but I have not seen any place where a road such as the *Azika* Way, of six traffic lanes with distinct divides from the multi-million naira international airport to the central square, will refuse to impress anyone. Children and housewives daily ignore the sidewalks and the first divide, reaching for the central partition to display carrots, oranges, lime and garden eggs. What a shame! Before you reach out to arrest them, they have jumped into the swift traffic and melt off, with their garden-egg baskets delicately balanced on their heads.

"The flower gardens bordering the sidewalks before the commuter lanes are now market grounds for festival rams and cows as well as sites for block moulding factories. We developed a separate unit to handle traffic congestion, with the prompt handling of careless and inconsiderate driving. As I was coming here, Sir, the ten-minute journey took more than two hours! I disembarked to walk the quarter of a kilometer to the artery of the fly-over at the *Upole* Army Resettlement Centre. To my greatest dismay, a *TKB* peugeot car had its engine completely dismantled right in the middle of the road, consequently narrowing the three lanes into one. I ordered the immediate arrest of the two roving roadside mechanics and towed off the car to our yard so as to get the traffic moving again. Few meters away from the spot, a gentleman, apparently distracted by a hawking team, hit my car. They were hawking pineapples garnished with coconut right on a four-lane highway.

"My General, Sir, imagine how many patients must have died in hospitals, how many business appoint-ments must have been missed, the level of wear and tear to roads and cars, the fuel burnt and the litter on roads from hawkers that posed the greatest menace to urban civilization. These are results of what decades of protests by everyone, and especially the political class, have made of our city. Protest movements and riots have taken the human element and compassion out of our people.

"When democracy all over the world is transforming into political concepts of envy, as you rightly observed in one of your speeches, Sir, we are still not aware of what a state must look like. Our people ignore government directives and move from one misjudgement to another and the idea..."

"Major Meno," the President cuts-in with a low voice. "I think that we are enjoying your level of understanding of the problems on hand. By your training you are supposed to be very thorough as an army engineer. But play home, Major. Now play home."

"Your Excellency, trying to bring this city to normalcy is no longer feasible. As I see it, only one of them, not operating in uniform and as relentless as Mahama Ghandi, can do the job. But for now, we can defeat this decadent and unwholesome system without a gunshot, drop of blood, litigation, and bad name for this administration or more money down the drains. This administration must revisit the decision of a past administration to move House to a new capital.

"Honestly, your excellency, we must say bye-bye to Lapas and get off the eyesore. A great country like ours needs a good and captivating environment to attract foreign investments in the productive sector and tourism.

If you will permit me to use the language, there is no enabling environment for the government to project its name and image in this city any longer. The tragedy of our existence is Lapas and we are the present day example of Biblical Babylon with abundant glory without trace. We can adjust, and this must be done now or never. Lapas is like Babylon, a city of wilful sinners.

"The present state of our psyche, and indeed the seat of our governance, must change before we can achieve any substantial growth with the mammoth resources available to us as a nation. The two past administrations spent billions on the new capital and in fact, the over-thrown civilian administration has been conducting skeletal government functions there. We must move out from Lapas, Sir.

"We may be called upon one day to host the world and Lapas is not a good venue for such. My General, Sir, you must revisit the issue of a new capital and continue where the past administration stopped. Under the new dispensation, I don't need more than a hundred men to ensure a good environment for the take-off of the new capital..."

"Is that a pledge, Major?"

"Yes, Sir. And I will carry out the pledge to the letter."

*   *   *

The broadcast came the next evening on the radio and television network. It was a speech laden with the usual stern looks and harsh voice characteristic of Baguludu, even with his tooth-full laugh on screen and newspaper pages.

"The efforts we have put into government these few months have been tremendous. If the achievements were to manifest, this administration would have been a great one; a regime ready to stand tall, beat its chest and challenge others to a success-record contest.

"However, Lapas is the headache. This wilderness of insanity is the trouble. This concentration of the most decadent in our nation is the issue and we must tackle it promptly. A colonial administrator warned this nation about Lapas over eighty years ago that ecological and man-made social dislocations were likely to make Lapas ungovernable before the turn of the century.

"Few months back, this administration set up a task force, principally to ascertain why Lapas was turning gluttonous concerning everything. The task force was to clear the rubbish that was the bane of Lapas and to re-orientate the people on the right attitude to urban facilities; to put a stop to the excessive abuses on infrastructure and, consequently, work out new strategies for the city economy to move ahead in the right direction.

"The futility of our idea and the money we daily sink into Lapas was lately revealed to us in a report by the committee which was submitted to the council of state indicating that Lapas was no longer redeemable. Consequently, this administration will have to take decisive steps by implementing, without further delay, the recommendations of the panel for the movement of the seat of government to the new federal capital as earlier recommended by a previous military administration. This administration has thus decided as follows:

1. To immediately move the seat of the government from Lapas to Amuta.
2. To move the first set of federal ministries and parastatals consisting of the cabinet office, foreign affairs, internal affairs, finance and defence to the new capital on the 1st of next month.
3. To release funds immediately from the federation account to facilitate preliminary work on the infrastructure needed and on which the last administration has made considerable commitment.
4. To appeal to everyone to have faith in our new capital and handle whatever role they are called upon to play with finesse and national commitment. These are needed to give our new capital a wholesome appearance. In reaching this decision, the council ... ”

*   *   *

"God Almighty! They have finally moved the capital. We thought they were just wasting resources on a place not to be inhabited," Aderera Aminu, the incumbent president of the *Isun-Osa Club* broke the stillness in the billiard room of the clubhouse where at least a dozen other members gathered. That ended the attention and the switch-off was swift; psychological and physical. He moved his massive frame from the high-back chair of the billiard room where, as the president, he had veto as in all games-room.

"So you're here," he identified retired Major Etim Allen who suddenly showed up at the billiard hall from the TV Centre.

"You heard what your General said? You boys are very powerful. I bow to you and tremble like a pilgrim at the holy shrine."

"Mr. President, when soldiers are in government, they are conjurers, constantly using history as trick," Major Allen flayed his former profession.

"I believe you, but how can you just move the seat of government like that... just like that! Lapas? This city has been capital for almost a century. In fact, since amalgamation. We thought they were building a capital that will not be used. A kind of retreat centre for government officials."

"Orders is orders, and you should be looking forward to the mad rush for contracts. Amuta will be our fourth capital. Actually, Lapas is congested, although it was the attitude of the people that congested it and not the forest of concrete and glass we created out of it or the volume of human traffic..."

"Major, that's not enough reason for them to move the capital to a jungle. Besides, the last government refused to act on the issue because of reports by a reputable world health body that the location was infested with parasites of lassa fever to which no known cure had been discovered."

"My President Sir. But your 'people' created Amuta," a voice interjected from another group of discussants at the far end of the billiard table. It was Usman Lash, upright and objective in his comments. Though not a

57

friend of government, Lash never opposed laudable initiatives.

"Barrister A.A. Aduga created Amuta. Lawyers! The only learned ones in this country, making and unmaking events. Even with our degrees, to them we are all illiterates. Mr President, Barrister Aduga was your colleague at the law school. Your *people* took the wind out of the sail of Lapas and why must anyone around here complain? They made a mess of a rewarding situation. I have never seen any group so fervently talented in crowd conspiracy with all its unpleasant trappings."

"His people"?

"Yes, Major. His *people*. He knows his people and they are as swift as the eagle in filing court actions. Just wait twelve hours more and their application will be before a judge, restraining the government from moving even a paper to Amuta. His *people*, they confuse issues a lot. My President, that's the truth and...."

"We are very detribalised in the Army," retired Major Etim cuts in.

"You see, no tribal sentiments in the army. You bloody civilians rake up sentiments and tribal jingoism. What is the issue about *people* here? Your intention probably is that ninety percent of the issues of a new national capital are concealed from people's understanding. You invited them to government and you must definitely pay for your foolishness and thoughtlessness."

"Lapas is a prodigy, my president. It is a practical example of a socialised pagan community, the African

58

version of Haiti. The social decadence is alarming and we have sufficiently painted ourselves to the world that decent dwelling meant nothing to us. I am one of the few who believe fervently that this facet of our psyche must change before we can achieve any substantial growth with the abundant resources available to us as a nation for the entire world to appreciate."

And that is the truth rammed into the system of members and it increased as the discussions dragged on. Lapas was actually a prodigy of a city and a nation's capital that lost glamour and grace, not because of over-population, environmental limitations or government neglect, but the attitude of the people to good and decent living, the instances of which are numerous.

"Our highly unhealthy living standard..." Major Etim resumed after a little gulp from his glass of beer, "...has made it too difficult for available facilities to cope. Karachi still lives and orders still endure in Beijing. But here, we have decided not to let anything work. The attitude of local indigenes itself is another issue. Every aspect of their behaviour points to the fact that they are destroyers, vagabonds and social misfits, in spite of their claims to early social contact with the whites before any other group nationwide.

"Shopping around the famous *Maras* Street is with hard labour and this is the spot where foreigners pick local batiks, crafts and high precision imported items for household usage. The *pressure boys* have taken over. They snatch necklaces, bracelets, handbags and briefcases. An ambassador's wife had it rough recently. She lost over two thousand dollars to the boys who snatched her handbag while trying to pay for a set of cane chairs. The *pressure boys* melted into the high rise refuse dump that has cut the road from motorists.

"Refuse and filth are another issue. Lapas is the dirtiest capital in the world. On any occasion, if the *pressure boys* permit, take an early ride round the city. Local government staff, working overnight, must have cleared all areas. Before ten in the morning, the hawkers, trading items from packaged fruit drinks, pure water, fast foods and raw food, must have littered the roads again! I personally saw a plantain fryer toasting her wares off, right in the middle of the road at the intersection of *Maras* Street and the *Marine* area. To her, it was normal. And her customers, including even the users of the three lanes she narrowed into one, did not see anything bad in it. She created confusion that everyone saw as normal to sustain living. And daily, quite ironically, a madman, sitting by the adjourning petrol station, eating from the trash and dressed in all rags with dangling sorts of metals and junk medals, stepped into the junction and gracefully controls the traffic. You will..."

"Major!" a member who had been raptly following cuts in.

"I felt sorry the day I saw that madman controlling traffic to ease the chaos created by sane men. God Almighty! He held a club aloof, bangs on your bonnet to stop you for traffic on the other side to move!"

"I am happy that you have also encountered one of the shames of Lapas. Nonchalantly, our people pass by to pick the toasted plantain, and walk pass the man that looked like devil in hell. More than a score police patrol and traffic control teams daily pass by him. To me, we all carry the same state of mind with that madman because we pretend to be mad on daily basis when the few sane ones talk reason around us.

"Time was, when we had Independence Square in this country, located in central Lapas as a symbol of our freedom. "A beautiful fountain giving up cool, clean water of six meters high in graciously inviting showers. Flowers, the much-respected princesses of the vegetable kingdom, displayed their beautiful plumes even when sunrays appear gluttonous. Suddenly, we moved in, and turned the fountain into laundry and open shower squares. Some hoodlums outwit each other to dismantle the pumping machines as rapidly as the government replaced them. Today, our fountain is nothing but an abode for fungi and spirogyra. We should all embrace this order and join the head of state to say bye-bye to Lapas."

The stillness of the room was infectious. A pin-drop silence as Major Etim turned the billiard room into a lecture theatre. He opened up much of the daily decadent practices in the city, seen as normal city habits, but highly damaging to the estimation in which the country was held and the goodwill entertained towards her. The *Isun-Osa Club* president gently moved from the oak door by which he rested his heavy frame, grabbed the snooker on the billiard table and placed it at the starting point, ready for a shot.

"Major! I was told you were a directing staff at the Staff College, teaching environmental and social studies, Course 211 they call it?"

"Far from it, my President. I was just at the Staff College as a military assistant to the commandant. I picked up random tutorial sessions but on strategic studies and arms limitation only. However, as an infantryman, I lay emphasis on enemy detection strategy by correct interpretation of signals, firepower accuracy, circular aero-probability and survivability in the event of an unexpected onslaught. I have lived in Lapas for many years both as a serving and retired officer. Hence my knowledge of the limitations of the city. Generally, I know this city. And more importantly, I know this country and I am proud of this".

"Your observations are right. I know a little part of this globe. I too, have travelled. To be candid, hardly have I seen a capital where things have been so messed up like Lapas. You know this is the only city in the world where there is no surviving housing estate. All highbrow living estates have metamorphosed into offices and shopping centers. The banks have bought over the descent houses and the new generation of skinhead bankers mill around for lunch concealing in their pockets, notes skinned off each of the packs of currencies paid out. It is part of the indecency that they are not in Lapas to merely 'see the bridges.' They finger off something from every payment made out, for their shirts to maintain their cassava level and for their ties to stand erect.

"You can pick a good tuber of yam or a fresh porcupine or African pangolin right at the gate of *Oke-Amun* Barracks? Drive them off this minute; the next minute when the Head of State has driven into his office, the baskets are on display again.

"The President of the World Trade Forum arrived at the Lapas Airport last month for a three day' visit. He was suddenly accosted by over three hundred hoodlums, the *pressure boys* as we call them, with bare chests and weird hair cuts as he stepped off the check-out counter. He ran back into the hall thinking that it was a crowd of demonstrators. The team that met him on arrival explained that they were just touts who were out to peep into people's wallets and bags.

"I think Lapas boys had succeeded in bringing the city from grace to grass before anyone recommended the movement. Streetlights are gone from the city. They were all fingered off at the dead of the night. The Police recently made an arrest of a Datsun panel van filled with stolen streetlight bulbs. At the rear screen was a sticker – *'I will make it'*. He actually made it into police custody."

"Are you sure the police really put him into custody?" a member inquired jokingly.

"Two hours later, the friend of the culprit feigned ownership of a burgled electrical bulbs shop around the area and demanded that the seized goods be returned to him. The Police said that since they did not catch him on pole tops, it was difficult to proof that the bulbs were actually removed from the poles and that release must be made so that the business of the man would not suffer. You could guess what the syndicate which got the goods out quickly from police custody did with the power of the naira, in order to meet supply deadline to the electricity board which issued the *LPO* for the supply of street light bulbs. Its own goods were re-supplied at a higher fee.

"Lapas, a city where the robbers are adulated and the robbed ones are stoned. A city where girls are constantly wanting to look like women and the women wanting to look like men." The president of Oke-Amun Club concluded sadly.

Well, these are some of the problems of Lapas. Who will then blame President Baguludu for his action? It became common knowledge later that at the cabinet meeting which ratified the decision before the broadcast, General Baguludu signed off Lapas as the national capital and distributed the rest of the golden pens to his ministers and service chiefs. An hour later, he flew out in the presidential jet, heavily guarded in the air by airforce fighter jets to resume duties at the new capital in Amuta. *Bye-bye Lapas, your glory and beauty are hereby discounted.*

order five, rule five

"...under the sky, everything is in the open"

If you believe in incantations, counter spells, charms and fetish concoctions, do not go to Drube. You will only be disappointed at the utter levity with which the potency of such human beliefs are treated. Drube is a town with a difference. Less than twelve kilometres to Amuta, the federal capital, Drube is the town of Major Bellah, a key putchist under the new dispensation and the state secretary for the new capital territory. It is an all Christian town adjourning river Dru, and the residents' early touch with colonial explorers changed things considerably.

Major Samson Bellah had told pressmen on assumption of office that the federal capital territory covered only a ninety-kilometre radius, cutting across five contiguous states, and not one hundred kilometres as published by previous administrations. His town of Drube fell off the hook of displaced original inhabitants by just ten kilometres.

"It was not my making. The original document is clear on ninety and not one hundred. If the civilisation of my people must be disturbed because of a national goal, no one can resist that. But Drube is not in the capital territory and I am inviting the press for a tour," Major Bellah had stoutly defended his small but highly historical village on the national television as criticisms mounted in the dailies as to how he was displacing settlers to make way for construction work at the capital while he cleverly excised his own village from the roars of bulldozers.

"I saw that village. No one will want that peculiar life-style destroyed," the editor of the *Daily Parrot* observed at the new National Press Centre to be commissioned by the head of state and on which a considerable government involvement was visible.

"In Drube, no one believed in mechanical or orthodox healing. Father Dan of the Drube Healing Home said orthodox healing begins only where spiritual healing fails. Devotion to God had put everyone in the realm of the spirit to the extent that the healing process, from just the common headache to psychiatric distresses, are done by prayers, an approach which they claimed never fails!"

"Mere prayers?" a colleague from the *Sun Times* asked sceptically.

"Ah, if you say that before Father Dan, he will start a cleansing session on you. He has warned us never to call prayers 'mere'. He made us believe that the reason behind the opening up of people to expel a disability is their failure to communicate effectively with their Creator. I don't believe Major Bellah, but I believe his people on the process of spiritual purification."

"I still don't believe any of them. Neither Major Bellah who has tampered with the lapses in the documents to keep his people on site to be able to enjoy the spill-over of facilities from a federal capital just ten kilometres away, nor his people who think that the alarming invasion of human propensity to live by invading bacteria and viruses can easily be waded off or controlled by prayer sessions. Maybe they are not aware of recent findings that the human body is made up of ten trillion cells which equally harbour one hundred million bacteria. I am not impressed at all."

"But, why must you be easily taken away by words from a soldier's mouth. Soldiers? Gooosh! They are aberrations. They talk to keep going and shoot their way to get to no particular destination; not caring about whose horse is gored. Soldiers are looters wherever they pop out their bayonets. They loot the treasury, the national psyche, the individual conscience and, before you know, they have looted you of your nationality. Never join them to steal, or to create and condone confusion, disorder and chaos on issues easily resolved by negotiation."

"Major Bellah has started his own looting. My fear is that when this nation has been institutionally dismantled and thoroughly ploughed, they must not forget to sow the massive landmass with corn! But we in the press will continue to press ahead." *The Sun Times* reporter closed his submission.

"You are a departure. A complete departure from the editorial policy of your paper. *The Sun Times* had always defended this government and even the one before it. Your paper, the radio and television through a national network kept them on board. You chart the course by your editorial policies and commentaries. As a reporter for a private newspaper, I don't have a lust for democratic rule as such. All noise about civil rule, democratic institutions, political dispensation are just tirades of mere literary excellence without political wisdom." John Mefon of the *National Flagship* drew a puff and stepped on his cigarette butt to ensure that it was completely put out.

"Methinks..." he resumed, "...that democracy is not even a good system in any society. It is as confusing and barbaric as it sounds. Great nations of the world today with unfailing infrastructure, reliable and efficiently working facilities have either gone through one autocracy or the other. Actually, I don't think that our people quarrel. No, not at all. Only the press which knows everything does the fighting. They fight an imaginary enemy and with the wrong weapon on daily basis. What we behold on our pages everyday is combative journalism, combating only for their own goodness and they operate more out of ignorance than patriotic fervency. Our sad experience in Africa and especially this country is that the press developed before the executive, judiciary and the legislature. By the inverted pyramid approach, the last became the first and has used its glamour to pull down laudable programmes, stall erudite initiatives and arouse negative reactions to all government initiatives. See what they are doing with Major Bellah now. The press, I am sorry to note, has brought more distresses to government than any other arm which... Oh sorry! The head of state or Mr. President is here. I am the master of ceremony. I must be at the dais."

The outriders were numerous. The sweep was clean. The *CCD* did its job to the last detail, employing the strategy of overwhelming response. The gathering of prominent journalists, high-ups and the government delegation was easily eaten up by the bevy of security men with assorted weapons. This probably played home the fact that the *C-in-C* was at the national press centre to *re-act* and conduct an operation with the necessary efficiency and speed hitherto stocked away in *The Rocks*, a grand feature of the new capital, after which the state house was named. Soldiers in peculiar tunic melted into the green surrounding bush. Every furniture and fitting at the centre was security-checked. A massive edifice in Brazilian architecture, it housed four conference rooms, an indoor sports hall, an editing studio, two bars, four chalets and thirty single-rooms and a modern lawn tennis court. The project was financed hook, line and sinker by the government."

The ovation that greeted the invitation of the military president to present his address was waived short by securitymen. General Ramos Baguludu rose swiftly on his feet, looked round and spotted the state house reporter for the *National News Agency*, winked at her and recoiled back into his usual stern looks.

"My colleagues of the press, I am not going to address you today. We are to talk to each other and reason together about our national psyche, the dangers in our national image, how they came about and those to hold responsible. We must also think of a solution". He looked at the President of the Journalists Council nodding countless frantic 'yes' to the opening remarks. The thunder was yet to strike.

"First and foremost, I must congratulate you for this beautiful Press House. I commend Major Bellah for the allocation of land. This press sanctuary is your castle forever, and you must use it to contribute to the building of a strong, rich and viable nation. Search through history, and you will discover that the press has never, and will never, operate as a Robinson Crusoe without a man Friday. Nations had needed the press to plan their growth while the press had constantly needed the government to have an enabling environment in which to function and keep up its image, prosperity and ethnic cohesion.

The plurality of the press in the country has not taken away its duty of first ascertaining that what is to be published conforms to national constitutional provisions and ethical standards. You will agree with me that press freedom is globally circumscribed because it is an antimatter capable of falsifying all truths. Complete freedom of the press is an absolutism that no government anywhere in the world can guarantee; not even when it is an emerging democracy like ours that needed little or no debate in laying the foundation for future advancement for children yet unborn and unbegotten. We have examples to follow and we will not debate the basic needs of the people before we provide them. We have no time to waste and you must understand this. We are no parliamentarians. Wait until those who know how to pile-up issues and deceive you will come to parliament.

"Proprietorial interests, government secrets and gratification syndrome, necessitated by poverty and habits, are some reasons why a realistic modification of the status quo is a hard but necessary labour. The Wilbur Scram theory needed to be amended. Scram in his *Theory of Mass Communication* did not envisage a multiplicity of societal actions and the current human drive towards acquisition of whatever is acquirable by any means." General Baguludu pulsed while catching the gaze of the national president whose initial nods had scaled into a fixture.

"Lies, misrepresentations, misquotes, confrontations and overt reactions to directives are some of the dangerous games the press love to play. Terrorist journalism is the vogue in this country, and the African foremost press is today holding the nation hostage. Little did you know, however, that success in journalism has nothing to do with wolf crying, character assassination, encouragement of national disorder and the global portrayal of our country, the most populated in the black world, as a pack of insincere and docile managers of politics and economy. Go round and see what we have raised out of a jungle, our unity city. To you, it is nothing. Bellah is to you a rogue, but is he? Everything about us is open, including the armouries. We have nothing to hide. We are in military service both in the barracks and the state house.

"Unbridled economic terrorism, currency slumps, divestment, collapse of commercial conglomerates are features of today's world economy. Survivability is by joint action. In fact, international economic terrorists have become actors in the international system, and all over the world, bread diplomacy is rife. But to the pressmen in this country, you register our cast and sound track more by portraying your country as a bunch of fraudsters or scammers. You never consider for a moment that if the business is in their national interest, then it is a good deal. If not, you help echo their grief and paint us as 419. The foreign press relies on what you write to fill their pages and airtime. Even foreign correspondents here present will rely on your sentiments as background to their reports. It is simply the case of a little surrogate instructing the big one!

"The mantle of leadership fell on the army by invitation, brokered by the politicians themselves. The army realised the fourth estate as necessary to enable the people understand the gradual necessity needed for our own type of system to endure. We will not copy. Never! We know what we want and we will not copy.

"Little did you all realise that we are business partners to our own enemies and we are mere large depositors into a bank of distrust and hate. The military merely became the victim of a double blind: local press hostility and foreign press ignorance. Little do you know also that this country's military is not just a mass sinew, fang and claw as you portray it to the public and the outside world? In the mad scramble to paint us black and blue, the lessons of development and the last civil war, which you were supposed to bring home to the people that started it, were lost and lost forever. If you know the enormity of fear, terror and despair in our past republics, you will daily justify our interference in governance positively to the outside world.

"Today you have all the good things of life to your credit. But you are unmindful of the fact that the military has brought the former four axis of development to thirty-one, including the new federal capital where you now sit to commission a sanctuary. By such increase, we today maintain the highest concentration of cities in Africa, resulting in the largest number of road network and the greatest concentration of tertiary institutions and media houses. In fact, ours is the largest communication network in the continent with almost a hundred radio and television houses. People of this nation know these. Only the press pretends not to know. Under the present national objective, the press is a television, very amusing to watch because of its excesses and idiosyncrasies. This country is crumbling not under the gun, but under the pen of those who have vowed to make her great. From yellow to junk, the press has matriculated into a high scale retailer of slander, libel and treason. It is an irony to note that the press that is supposed to know that government actions are not conducted on the pages of newspapers, openly and on daily basis reduced the estimation of government in the minds of the world by their spate of scurrilous writings and negative banner headlines.

"Mr. President of the Journalists Council, some of your papers have recently gone off the curve; they think that they are foreigners here. How do you place an editor who captioned his story; *'It is Finished!' 'Break Up Now,' 'Baguludu's son May be Disabled,' 'This Country is Gone.'* There are countless others committed world-wide daily to celluloid memories tending to indicate that the programme we are pursuing is a deceit. Journalism is today a national cancer, always bringing rot into our national soul. Government judged those before you. You will also be judged. And we are on our way. The decree to this effect is in the pipeline."

General Baguludu covered almost half the distance to the Press House foyer to cut the tape and declare the house open before the reality dawned on the audience that he had concluded without the promised dialogue.

"I hereby declare this complex, which is to a journalist what a mess is to an army officer, open with additional token of ten million naira to..." the ovation was thunderous. The razor-sharp edges of his *number one* uniform, rather than protocol, prevented the president of the Journalists' Council from hugging him. He lifted the scissors and neatly cut the tape between the points of two pull ribbons.

"...to the glory of God and the use of man, particularly for the enhancement of a national course for growth, stability and understanding." The ovation rent the air again.

*   *   *

"Have you thought about the logic behind lies and the elegance of their designs by the press?" the director of legal matters in the foreign affairs ministry, Mr Adula Koma, asked the President of the Journalists Council at the cocktail after the departure of President Baguludu.

"My learned friend, putschists will always justify their actions. And it is not all the time that the reality of their intentions catches up with their rhetoric. What we listened to was a gluttonous rhetoric that meant just only one thing: continued military hold on national politics. Nothing more, lawyer. Nothing at all."

"So he didn't touch you at all?"

"With the donation yes. But with the tirade, no. They cannot play *God* with satanic intervention and still refuse to allow for checks and balances. That's what the press is doing which lawyers cannot do. The day the army seized power was the day all peace but one died. The press is that last one hope for the restoration of life, peace and ambition. After years of independence; freedom and democracy as well as self-determinism are still largely elusive. We have been enslaved by our own creation. The army merely glorifies in the conception of grand plans for an ideal economy, ideal political climate and ideal social environment while they loot the treasury successively," the writers' president looked angry.

"But you share in that loot. The splendour of this building, the figures on this cheque, all point to the fact that journalists are pen contractors. We hear of letters to the editor, have you ever heard of letters to judges? All that we want is an ideal state, based on justice and reason, even when brought out from the barrel of the gun; it must be a succeeding process from democracy to democracy. I think that journalists and soldiers are guilty of a similar offence: the betrayal of national goal: and robbery of the national conscience with the pen and the gun. That's the only game the two of you love to play. Henceforth, I think, we must be very sceptical about your *parker* and their *fabric nationale*."

"My learned friend, don't you know that the criminal and the innocent all need the media? We create the terrain suitable for contest for you lawyers who rush into politics just for the gains. Our bold headlines, stories and features sing your ideals to seek the office. Maybe the press should allow the office to seek the man and not the man to seek the office any longer. Maybe press involvement in political change must have its limits. Maybe we have to ..."

"Mr President of Journalists, what the head of state is saying is that falsification of all truths and half truths is not in the nation's interest. Journalism should be devoid of lies, rumours, slanders and character assassinations, and national cannibalism should be discouraged. The United States didn't destroy her presidents and prominent nationals to be a world power. Britain didn't, and France never tried it. The press must no longer create a store-house of horror which will scare future generations and make them see justice as revenge against a section of the country or against an arm of government."

*   *   *

It was a carrot and stick treat. A cheque of millions of naira on one hand and a slam of long-drawn orders on the other. The orders in Decree 49 were the worst to happen to the press since the colonial times. It was specifically conceived to muzzle the press. It covered excesses from photojournalism, letters to the editor, story write-ups and features to editorial opinions of whatever shapes or forms:

* No journalist shall take, process or publish the unofficial picture of any government functionary, without prior approval from the state house or the relevant supervising ministry, failing which the journalist or medium shall be guilty of an offence punishable by a jail term of six months or fifty thousand naira in the alternative.

* Any picture culled or reproduced from a previous material, either foreign or local, but which tends to lessen the estimation of the government or any of its functionaries in the mind of the right thinking members of the public shall constitute an offence similar to the above and similar sanctions shall be applied.

* Any publication of falsehood and inaccurate report of government statements, functions and court proceedings shall be deemed to be a culpable action, and the reporter guilty of an offence and liable to twelve months imprisonment without an option of fine.

* Any unfair comment, distortion of historical facts and details to achieve an editorial objective and seen or determined by government as malicious, shall constitute an offence punishable by twelve months imprisonment without an option of fine.

* Any comment, debate, vox pop or analysis considered to be in further pursuance of private interest at the expense of government or any of its functionaries shall be considered as offensive and punishable by the closure of such a media house for a period of six months in the first instance.

* No point of privilege, either qualified or absolute, shall hold in the determination of the extent of guilt in any of the cases. Identification of defamatory or seditious matter, either by innuendo òr expressly stated, against a journalist, media house or media body which this Decree 49 simply refers to as a *Media* shall be upon the mere production of the material of publication in court.

* Any media house so closed shall recommence publication after appropriate penalty has been served, by additional payment of a re-registration fee of five hundred thousand naira only, a surety in the person of a high government functionary or reputable private individual to the tune of the same amount.

* Henceforth, no newspaper, magazine, radio, periodical or any other publication or broadcast, carrying items of information, shall be published for sale or consumption, without the payment of a mandatory registration fee of three hundred thousand naira only. Such registration rights shall be withdrawn if the government feels reasonably satisfied that the

right of publication has offended public decency. The right of withdrawal is not subject to challenge by any reporter, editor, editorial board, proprietor or any vendors' association.

* It shall be an offence...

The new press sanctions looked endless. But it ended, although not with pleasant platitudes. The regime was prepared to enforce every sanction if the decree is violated. The Army's 2nd Division at Lapas was consequently upgraded to a composite division. This was to enable it to cope with all emergencies at the former capital, still largely functioning as the country's commercial hotbed and political arena from where most of the newspapers and the few private radio stations already on air as a result of deregulation, operated. Lapas was a city with no industrial parallel nationwide, though it was lacking in social, health and environmental decency.

order six, rule six

"...everyone has a right to be wrong, including the right to die!"

It was a festival of political impasses. Politicians from all nooks and crannies of the country had been pre-programmed with the images of confusion. They hardly thought right, talked right or behaved right about the democratic way forward. The take-over by the military was a take-over of their political potency. It was a period of baby-boom politicians whose plans were merely to shout their way to power through appointments in an unofficially adopted diarchy. It was a record time for political blunder, by a class of the society that failed to organise itself rationally for a good contest, to hold on to power. Great strides at very opposite directions with individual politicians competing for attention to sell his own slanderous wares against the other, daily filled the pages of almost the twenty newspapers retailing sedition, nationwide.

The ram on their conscience and disorderly behaviour was most appropriately applied at the graduation of the latest set of redneck officers from the Military Staff College. The Army Chief of Staff, Lieutenant General Koni Piyam, who represented Mr. President, was noted for his excellent oratorical power and delivery.

"We have relentlessly tried to bring military rule to a close in this country, but the disorder and lack of

seriousness latent in the political class have often constituted the impediment to handing over to this set of
unorganized and highly undisciplined bandits called:
'politicians'. The consequence, you will believe, is that
our professionalism has been greatly affected with all
efforts concentrated on state duties rather than defence
and security. Today, we restate again and we must not
deceive ourselves, that the ultimate ambition of every
soldier is not to be a General or Field Marshal. Rather,
it is to be a governor, minister or head of state. This, in
practical terms, is a negation of our commission."

The shuffling of ceremonial khakis was rocking the
hall already and the gorgets showed brightly on many
collars.

"This is why we always have coups and counter
coups. Power is often very beautifully horrifying that
its possessors try to personalise it and eventually find it
difficult to relinquish. The situation is not different for
the military. The added advantage to our continued
hold on power is that in democracy, every one has a
right to be wrong, including even the right to die.
Contending parties in democracy must *war-war* rather
than *jaw-jaw*. In the military, no one has a right to be
wrong. In Germany, during the Second World War,
boys of fifteen were manning anti-aircraft guns and
they had no right to make mistakes, because their
orders were specific about enemy planes. They had no
right to leave such duty to a future generation that
might be neither giants nor Samsonites. In the military,
we talk to agree and give our orders to specifics. Cannons
respect cannons and not the subterfuges of conferences,

platitudes and the invocation of sentiments in which politicians pride themselves. They never agree to act in concert because of reckless individual ambitions and hidden agendas that are not usually in conformity with party ideologies.

"Give the platform to the military to negotiate democracy, no common grounds will ever exist between the bullet and the ballot. One is freely given; the other is forcefully obtained as an instrument of intimidation. We cannot negotiate to give democracy. It will be freely given and freely taken when the receivers decide to make themselves available and are prepared to receive it. The cliché that democracy is not negotiable means more to us than to the politicians. No one may negotiate the sun off its course on the rotational axis of the earth, but the earth itself knows that it must appropriately and concisely rotate at that axis to enable the course of day and darkness to take their due. The people are very honest in their choice of inviting the military to take over power, and we will not introduce a tracing-paper approach and panic measures to restore democracy.

"Since 'self' and 'national deception' entered into our national politics, and pessimism became the scale for recording our movement, politicians have often grinned from ear to ear like warring officers in 'Daddy's Army', with a view to scurrying favour for position. The tenacious greed of our political leaders has rocked the boat of democracy, at least for now, as you must have known that all political arrangements before we came to power were made, not for the convenience of the people, but for the comfort of those in power.

"In politics, you are involved to be given a position, while in the military, you are there to serve at the risk of your life. The military will never, I repeat, never be goaded into handing over power in a chaotic set-up and we will not require less than four years more to put a new democratic structure in place. We daily grapple with the duty of *statecraft* and *milicraft* and, as such, must not be rushed by any group parading itself as genuinely interested in democratic changes when they are, in real terms, the greatest opponents of a lasting democracy. With careful planning to be manifested in a staggered agenda for handing over, ours will be the last military coup and regime in this country. We cannot be definite on the category of those that will succeed us out of the present crop of sly politicians, uncircumcised analysts and the pathologically unrepenting moneybags who drew the nation back a decade when they had the opportunity to be in power. But we know those on who our focus is fixed.

"A rush out will be golden to those who are never contented with the 'win or lose' spirit of sportsmanship. This has been the guiding principle in politics for centuries, but they are always ready to lure junior ranks into another coup each time they are kept out of power. Our steps will be with caution."

Lieutenant General Piyam was enjoying the rapt attention of listeners at the venue. The pin-drop silence was worth it, for the issue was one of the most widely debated within the military, the civil service it subjugated and the political class that daily sang like canary about the illegal hold on power by a few using the instrumentality of state meant for other priorities.

"I don't see why the political class thought that it knew more than the military in the multi-dimensional ways of building this country," he resumed again.

"No country has achieved greatness without a measure of autocracy, totalitarianism and fascism. I challenge any one to make such a list public. China had her own foot of stone on the ground when decisions being enjoyed today were made. Soviet Union had her own fair share of iron hold on government to build a solid state. France kept a little freedom off the people to be able to build Paris before inviting the world to see the city, and thereafter die, if they so wished. The period of the Lords in Britain was one when governance was lorded over everyone to enable the structures we now rush there to enjoy to be put in place. The United States fought a terrible war to make the world love America. We always postpone our own sacrifice of freedom by copying the freedom level in Europe and America.

"Besides, our attitude to life, situations, structures and the affairs of state in Africa, is such that a little regimentation is necessary to enable us achieving our objective for development. Our politicians, indeed the entire black world, know nothing about the essence of government. Their idea is that government is used to fatten our personal treasuries, vilify the opponent, oppress the poor and refurbish the silver linings on the pillows of the rich. No! The diarchy we operate, instead of a pure military state, is an indication that we wish to carry everyone along in the process of building a viable state. You don't have to be a minister, governor, general or commissioner before you can help build your country. Money is nothing, commitment is the principal thing.

"In fact, building a stable state, which everybody will thereafter aspire to rule and buffet, does not come easy. No one experiments with it or turns it into a lecture series to train and convince people to stay...!"

At last he ceased fire and all other conclusions became *NTBB*.

*   *   *

"Ah! General meant business today. Na wah!" a major remarked as he got his beret off the hanger at the mess lobby.

"This one is another '*Sermon on the Mount*'. All officers must see it as the official reaction to the volume of bad blood generated, by military involvement in politics, among these bloody civilians. Give them power today, tomorrow they will mismanage and the next day, they are looking for a major to sponsor for a coup. *Chei, yeye people! Dem no dey think self.*" His commanding officer at the Physical Education Corps, Lt. Col. Yuba Sakai, threw in a few words before he sealed up himself in the cool comfort of his official, peugeot car, closely followed by a *V8* rover jeep.

The importance of the message, the occasion for delivery and location, Staff College, the nursery of high-rank power grabbers, made the media coverage enormous. But it did not go down well with the political class that was largely berated. Telephone calls, diverse and spooky, criss-crossed the nation for exchange of views, analysis, assessment and decisions on the mode of reactions. As usual, politicians will never let anything slipby without a wildcat noise making.

It was a good season for the press, highly noted for the nascent absurdities of watching news it could not *tell*, or telling the ones it didn't *watch*. Some *punched* the simple story directly into the state house and the *'Temporary'* ones gave it a hammer of colourful garb.

The front-page comment of *The Mirror* two days later was the anti-matter. It was a scurrilous sermon from another mount, a colourful confrontation that was not disguised. *The sudden anti-democrats,* as the paper titled it, was to set the new pace for new orders, both tall and short, but all serving as deterrents. It was what everyone referred to as a *'southpaw piece'*, so labelled because of the newspaper's proprietor's trade-mark of writing very powerful editorials with his left hand.

"Suddenly in this country, we have become permanent irritants to those who must worship and adore us as their *benefactors,*" the editorial opened in a mournful glee.

"Suddenly, we have become the antithesis of all rational behaviour, just because we always behave to endorse a commitment to orderliness. Suddenly, our politicians, without exception, have become pivots of forces that we must fight against. In the most inappropriate use of the word, the highly dedicated and peace-loving people of this country have been tagged and generally portrayed as 'anti-democratic elements' by a small group in starched uniform that overthrew democracy. What an irony!

"Irony is of divine origin, sharing the same top-down geometrical lineage with history. For as history records, man has constantly built structures of stone. But ironically, the docile and the ignorant loafer had always set off explosives of high payloads at the basement, shattering the fortunes of millions and drawing back the hands of the clock by a full cycle. The constant excuse is that the concrete mixture rebelled against the theory of solidity. This is our bane, as brought about by the military with a propensity and insatiable obsession to do another person's job all the time. The problem of the khaki boys is similar to that of a listener to a music who may intelligently pick the mistakes in the music, but who often failed to realize the mistakes in his own behaviour to the music. The military will never listen to right their own wrongs, which abound plentifully.

"These princes in power have indeed produced a cacophony of ironies and other African nations now punctuate their emerging democracies with panaceas, fall-outs and lessons from our own scornful and constantly cascading democratic arrangements. To those who look forward to our giant size for useful lessons, they are merely bequeathed with democratic babbling caused by the military. Everything in conscienceless militarism and indecency stare us in the face, while the carnival of political impasse created by military ineptitude, is discussed in every way except the right way. Now the military has created the situation to discuss it and the discussion has rightly began.

"When honest citizens of this country complain genuinely, our princes in power see such complaints as a senseless gloating that must not be weighed against our present state of political, economic and social squalor. The military clay-footed our growth for over thirty years and are still merchandising in group slander that we are not ready for governance. *Militarinomics* has failed, bringing with it a high level of unemployment, inflation, social dislocation, poverty, homelessness, corruption and countless ruinous alternatives. How we wished they cared about this and not the morbid ambition to become governors, generals and heads of state. They even went ahead now to call themselves military presidents. How awful?

"We have, with oneness of purpose and national patriotism devoid of irredentism, gone to the polls to elect our choices, only to be chased out of the state house with guns. What an irony! Military politicians are foxy in their attitude to national issues. Like the hedgehog, they know too many things but failed to know one big thing, which is that nations in the world thrive only on the pedestal of democracy. Just a parastatal in government is constantly gerrymandering to derail our national goals and paths to international honour.

"The confusion in their minds makes whatever institutions they build up for democracy a lethal trajectory, aimed at destroying those that democracy was meant to salvage and protect. Ours is a nation where *the rock* is for only those who can force their way through its highly fortified checkpoints. They get there and impose near impossible conditions for intending democratic choices of the people because of an erroneous idea that no military regime stays less than ten fruitless years in office.

"The time is now for all forces of democracy to save this nation from bleeding to death through the bayonets of a gang of khaki princes and looters of the treasury. Already, the country is all bone from head to the toe. Happily, however, our eyes can still see in the bare bone suckets. The *FN* may roar, the *Apache tanks* may boom, but the resolve will not melt. Happy days will be here at the end!"

*   *   *

The press secretary did his job well, at least to the official suffocating limits, by promptly cutting the incisive editorial with comments for the attention of the President. General Baguludu himself, even when he puts his foot in the mouth, he does not often put his hands completely in his pockets. He lashes out frequently at the meanest of provocation, the usual fashion and passion of military heads. If the press secretary's mind was bogged stiff by his perception of the military in politics, consideration for his bread and butter is often a deterrent to public pronouncements. To him, military heads in government secretariats are just seven-day wonders to behold. Uninformed nitwits, administrative dead woods and good-for-nothing intruders, the military are a whimsical desperation, rather than inspiration outside the barracks. This is so, not because they are totally ill equipped, but because of the consummate ambition for leadership and the absence of any social contract with the people they intend to lead to development. How many military heads of state ever swore publicly to a national oath of allegiance?

Insha Allahu ! Insha Jesus! *I will never lie,* are facades of blown-out lies and rhetorical misadventures in military governance. *Corrective Regimes* are coinages often turned into weapons to coerce and restrict. Uniform politics eventually becomes another human political theatre, with a cast of a kind and the brute force of nothing but a brute.

To derail the electoral process, you never had to be litigious or exploit the loopholes in the electoral law or the constitution. Just a few rifles and some combat gear, and you have forced your way through the air waves and, '*I, General, Rag, Tag, Tat Tat again...*' cements the treason in a few minutes with reckless orders rolling out like guns and ammunition from an armoury. What is the business of the military in government? Truly, why must a parastatal in the ministry of defence, an arm of government, be more powerful than the ministry and indeed the entire government? Why? If the military is a created instrument, then the instrument must necessarily be less powerful than the creator. The military arose out of the need for combat readiness against internal insecurity and to ward off external aggression when necessary. No other mandate outside this is constitutional and valid. The police force maintains law and order as a separate instrument of the police affairs ministry. There are countless others in this category. Those willing horses and aggressors of individual privacy, the radio and the television, momentarily shelve their heavy dosages of undeserving obscenities to get us informed that 'they' are here again. And they go no farther. They do not even attempt to analyse the persons behind the coups, their suitability to lead, their propensity to live up to national aspirations and the promise to make life more abundant.

Theirs is just to get the people merely informed through a ceaseless martial music and regular broadcasts of distasteful promises. But there are worse things than just being informed. Even with the high tendency to misinform and mis-educate, they still function solely as parastatals under the information ministry with their transmitters, like the guns, forming a veritable instrument for regicide. In essence, the national radio can take over government by a single broadcast, since a *coup d'état* itself is more of a sociological phenomenon than a muscular or gun booming affair! Afterall, many coups have succeeded without firing a shot, but the mere shuffling of jungle hats, boots shining knuckles, few uncorked riffles and some dry orders.

If every parastatal must take over government, each pledging to be more patriotic than the other, the fear looms large that there will be no inch of territory to take over at the turn of the century. Take-over broadcasts, meant to restate unsolicited commitments to corrective initiatives, do not often go into the diaries of cherished memories, as they are rich only in artlessness and purely barren of any articulated identification of worthy goals for advancement.

The press secretary in doing his job, was just thinking right, although too silently and toothlessly. The pen is like conscience, merely prickly and scratching while the guns boom, roar and compel. The president's comment on his press cutting was scanty but pregnant: *Eagle Claw*! The paper must not be allowed to run the concluding part the next day.

"Eagle Claw! God Almighty! This is for the military assistant to build another bridge of fists!" the press secretary was frantic as he moved to effect the execution of the order. A new way to damage the reputation of the military in the press by some combat-ready boys, always in top form to react or over-react to orders. As an obedient servant, he promptly passed the directive to the appropriate quarters.

"Another long watch, Sir! A war-war game and the president's order is specific to the effect that the seal up must be immediate," the military assistant was immediately on line to the *CCD* commandant for the proper execution of the order.

"You are to waste no time. The paper is about to go to bed and the continuation of that editorial must be stopped. Storm the premises with just a section. The mobile unit of the police force will complement your men with a truckload from *MOPOL 100*. Arrest the editor, his deputy and confiscate the next issue, or the bromide if the paper is still awake. The siege on the premises is indefinite! O.K? Those boys must have gone to hiding by now, but if you cannot get them, get their wives. They will surely show up!"

"*Oga, these journalist boys no dey marry o!* If we can't get their wives and we even discover..."

"Major! Tell the president that you have the men and equipment to perform your duty, but you cannot go ahead because the editor has no wife! Understand?"

"Sorry, Sir! I am on my way, Sir, on your orders," the commanding officer bellowed on the noisy handset at the other end; a foolish man trying a yell with a slashed throat.

"Make no mistakes. These are the orders of the C-in-C! Didn't you read the editorial? It is simply a misadventure and a blatant civil affront on the military. They have *mirrored* the wrong image of the military for too long. Let us see what they will now *mirror.*"

"Yes Sir! Over and out."

True enough, the order was to keep the *Mirror* away from the streets for eight months. The whole nation vividly remembered the vow to tamper with the press.

order seven, rule seven

"...you live at the edge of the grave and will soon tumble inside"

"This is a carrot-and-stick game. He gave millions with one hand and shut a newspaper house with the other," the editor of the *Daily News* observed as the news editor passed the story for his attention.

"Bastard or neat measure, Sir?" the news editor sought clearance on layout pattern as he coughed through the newsroom crowd in a halo of cigarette smokes, typical of a nightclub scene.

"Try bastard, across one, across two. Run to page six where we are running the story on human rights abuses from the world body. This is abuse in action."

"We must use every word of the story, Sir. In fact, it is a *'para-dey-go'* story. That is, a well-written eyewitness account from location. The invasion account is very detailed and this edition will sell, Sir. One of the soldiers was said to have even wondered why a newspaper must be called *The Mirror* when all that he knew is that a mirror is a looking glass. Funny guys, they never went to school. But I think we can run an editorial on the invasion, Sir?" the chief-sub sought clearance.

"Ah! That's a good idea, but all lead writers are off duty for the weekend. I have just passed the editorial for tomorrow to the composing room. Just dress your story well and go to town. Give it a background at the last but few paragraphs, for people to read between the lines. I think we are fine with that. Just mind your pitch."

"That is essential. Sir, you remember that tomorrow is the Armed Forces Remembrance Day. We must not do anything capable of being considered as an incitement. The sermon at the inter-denominational service after the parade is to be delivered by the Catholic Pontiff, Bishop Joshua Lubaba. We are sure that the man will roar," the news editor observed.

"What a wrong choice?" the editor intoned.

And it was indeed a wrong choice, never to be made again. If it had been left to the army chaplain, maybe such an open report on military rule and the undisguised call on politicians to revolt would not have taken place. Bishop Lubaba gave a political sermon, and not the expected soothing words to calm the pains in the hearts of those who lost their colleagues and relations in past wars.

*   *   *

"A soldier is an aberrant, and it is unfortunate that our own soldiers have refused to realise that they are merely majoring in the minor. They should be doing what they are doing here today, and nothing more. Beautiful parades to remember their fallen heroes, precise salutes and compliments to honour superiors, proper maintenance of our armaments and arsenals for combat readiness to defend our national integrity. But the military has strayed off its mandate and it is now groping in the darkness and wilderness it finally found itself," the catholic pontiff opened his indicting sermon. If they knew, they would not have called him to officiate. He was an ecumenical diary of national events and he had reasons for trying to monitor everything.

"According to Prophet Haggai, *'you have sown much and brought out little. You eat, but you have not enough. You drink, but you are not filled with drink. You clothe yourself and the people, but there is none warm. And under you, he that earneth wages earneth it to put it into a bag with holes.'* Then why are you still in government when your best is not good enough to make the people happy? Why? According to Prophet Haggai, you must *'consider your ways.'* Concentrate more on your normal calling. Stop majoring in the minor."

'The more you look for much to please the people,' Prophet Haggai has said, *'the more it came to little and even that little, the Lord did blow away.'* Why? You may ask. The Lord said it is because *His* house, this country, is in waste and that you have made everyone a prisoner of his own conscience. Consider your ways. The Lord asks in chapter two verse three of that book of Prophet Haggai: *'Who among you military leaders here present saw this country in her first glory? And how do you see it now? Is it not in your eyes, in comparison with the old, as nothing? 'Consider your ways.'"* Bishop Lubaba removed his glasses, surveyed the foyer and was vividly touched by the remorse pervading the entire gathering of top military rednecks, the officer corps and other ranks. It was an opportunity brought about by God to talk the reality into the ears of everyone. He was applying the

account of captivity by Haggai to illustrate how the army held the nation captive.

"The Lord said that *He* will shake this nation and listen to her desire, and allow this to pass and thereafter fill the country with glory and that this latter glory shall be greater than the former. This former glory is the military rule, which you may have considered to be the best. *'Consider your ways.'* Allow the Lord to take control of the destiny of this nation.

"It does not require hostile agitation and ceaseless protest to enthrone democracy in this country. According to my vision, the love of many for change in this country has waxed cold because of the indifference of the military, the hurdles and deterrents you put before them. You must consider your ways. You can't know more than the Lord who said *'I am in my Holy Temple, let the world keep silent before Me.'* Your action constitutes an affront on God and you may even want *Him* to vacate *His* throne for you. I am always startled and deeply worried on why you delight in finding solutions to problems by yourselves."

The mood was becoming too readable as to the nature of the sermon, but the Bishop was not done yet.

"Your ceaseless lies to the people cause you to stumble always, for the Lord said in *Amos 3:6* that *'shall there be evil in a city and the Lord not have done it?'* Liars will never inherit any stable government and the sanctions of God are clear: *'As you increase in your ranks and regimes and pile up your sins, therefore will I put the glory of everyone of you to shame.'*

" 'As you forsake the law of God for the good governance of my people, I will also forsake your children. They shall eat and not have enough. They shall commit whoredom and shall not increase. They shall fly in the skies and crash on the plains. They shall...' "

"grrrrrrrggrrrrrrrrrrrr.........gbam.........gbam.......gbam."

The national anthem rolled to live and the president and the service chiefs were on their feet, taking the final salute to bring the ceremony to an abrupt end. Bishop Lubaba threw both hands up and stood his ground, wondering what madness went into the army band. The *SPG* commandant briefly eyed the bishop as he threw all necessary machinery into gear for the president's exit.

The *C-in-C* was very troubled. He gave the order for the anthem. "You just turned the opportunity of your calling to pour venom on what you think is military adventurism. Why, my Lord Bishop? Why?" the army chaplain, Colonel Sunday Usman, was fretting.

"They are words from the Lord. I cannot do otherwise or the curse will be on me. I have no regrets for upsetting anyone. Rather, I am glad that I said what I was told to say, but not too glad that I was unable to finish with the consequences of their refusal to consider their ways. But as a chaplain, you know what I am saying. You are a soldier for Christ and counsellor for the people."

"You mean there is still more to say?" the chaplain asked, bewildered.

"Plenty, chaplain. Plenty, and I think I better do the rest through a press conference. I cannot play Jonah with God's message. It must be delivered even if I have to die thereafter. I saw the *SPG* commander pointing at me before he zoomed off with the president, and I know that his boys will nibble through loopholes to get me, but I am not bothered. This task is herculean and sacred, coming by inspiration from God. I am just an instrument for the delivery and I must not fear man to disobey God. No! Chaplain. No! Tell your commander-in-chief to learn to listen and not to treat all messages as anti-establishment, and see establishment itself as just only the military."

"But that was too sharp, my bishop. State affairs are not conducted that way. The pulpit must be used purely for sermons and not for political tirades against the government. With this sermon, some officers are likely to lose their jobs."

"Remember Alexander Pope who said; 'statesman, yet friend to truth; of soul sincere, in action faithful and in honour clear; who broke no promise, served no private ends; gained no tithe and lost no friend.' In the art of statecraft, how well does this apply to the military? Those wishing to be statesmen must live by the ideals of statesmanship. To the military and their generals, public trust is an irritant and this is why honesty in our national life is an endangered species," Bishop Lubaba was now by his car.

"Sir, I am afraid you are mixing ideals with reality."

"Let us wait and see."

*   *   *

During military regimes, newsreels maintain a ceaseless flow like spring water. They keep the military busy and the politician panting in their attempt to keep the pace set by the press. On this occasion again, the papers had a field day in their next editions with different versions and angles to the story of the Remembrance Day', the sermon by Bishop Lubaba and the abrupt end of the ceremony. The *Daily Arrow* got the background of the story and the paper gave it prominence as back page lead in bold caps; *'I AM NOT DONE YET.'* It confirmed that the bishop was to address a press conference to conclude his message. But the conference was never held as the order from the inspector general against unlawful assembly was dryer than the expectations of many..."

The beefy guy, in a wide shouldered suit, the type that gave no allowance for mistakes in cover-ups, arrived at the church hall, venue of the proposed press conference, at a little after eight in the morning. The way his left hip contoured, expressly confirmed that he carried a *Makarov* in a holster beneath his jacket. The church secretary wasted no time with his questions but promptly called out Bishop Lubaba to attend to his visitor.

"Sir, I am CSP Bayo Molekwu. Your press conference cannot hold. I have orders to inform you not to show up at all at the venue. My orders are definite, Sir, and there is no plan to embarrass you if you co-operate. I have just a small column of boys outside with just small arms, and that's all. Do not panic, but do not be funny in your cassock."

"Well, I don't plan to co-operate, and there is nothing funny about this country, my young officer. All I plan to do is to tell the world a message and this I must do either in cassock or in mufti. You shut down a newspaper house and made the people jobless when General Baguludu is operating from an illegal position of strength, and we must not say what God has asked us to say and see if the military can right the wrong?"

"No, Sir. By my orders, you are not permitted." CSP Molekwu roared, just at the same time a *Puma* attack helicopter hovered past the Church House.

"And you are in the skies too?" the bishop was bewildered.

"Just a few men up there, in case, sir. A few more arms also for reinforcement. Do not panic. Just obey orders. And if I may also add, I have pockets of reconnaissance men prowling around, Sir. You may mistake them for *pressure boys*, but they are effectively on duty. Don't attempt to smuggle the scripts out, just hand them over to me."

"Then you can as well stay at the harbour with a frigate, just in case also. You are even making more stories than I intend to make of God's message. You have again attempted to overshadow God. You are staging a coup against God. Just a press conference and you are assembling such a level of men and armament? The military government often presents itself as a bundle of overbearing stalwarts and I now see why this regime struck and came to power on an All Fool's Day. Fools! That's what you boys are. I am sorry. Fools!"

"No problems, my Lord Bishop. You know that this is a very tolerant government. We don't mind names or how and why we are called. If we mind that, our cells will be full by now. What we are indifferent to is the refusal to carry out orders. I am specific on my own orders, Sir. No press conference!"

Copies of Bishop Lubaba's scripts eventually went to the press houses later in the day, and with the circumstances surrounding the cancellation of the press conference, coupled with the long wait by journalists, the press gave more sympathy to the story. It was baffling to the inspector general who was assured that all scripts had been recovered and destroyed at the *SPG* Command Headquarters. How some of his officers handle matters of great security implications very often baffled him and he always hollered on his *DIGS* and *AIGS* during the weekly briefings of very senior officers.

As a man who rose through the ranks, he was merely playing the pot calling the kettle black. When files on cases of high criminal nature could walk their ways out of fire-proof safes, and hardened criminals could break steel bars in detention, walking through the charge counter to freedom; then talks about mere speeches slipping to the press are normally not treated as a punishable offence. It is just a case of applying the drug through the mouth when everyone knew where the pregnant woman must deliver her baby. IGP Okoh Fatunlah knows all but, as usual, would always put the blame of any dereliction on under-funding when defending the police in the public.

"Nobody teaches you how to do it, you learn the tricks on the job," he told the officers the next morning during a briefing, when the AIG zone four asked him how he was going to defend the police from the slipshod action and the failure to ensure that the script did not get to the press.

"Every man desires honour in and out of his home as the police need honour both with the government and the people. The president knows that if senior officers give firm orders, the rank and file who carry out the orders may add fairness to the firmness. Mr. president must understand that our honour must be intact or else the people will take the laws into their hands. Besides, the boys are poorly paid you know, and this is the issue I take up with the commander-in-chief regularly; and he has asked me to raise a memo to council on this. We are under-funded! I am representing him at the symposium on *Broken Homes and their Effects on Children*' organized by the Fair Treatment for Women Programme *(FTWP)* opening this morning at the conference centre. I intend to enlighten him more during my brief after the symposium," Mr. Fatunlah tried to defend the action of his boys.

How right is the claim that the police is under-funded? Or is it that the police lacked the excusable accounting discipline like the three arms of the military. If given the entire budget of the military, which will pay salaries, buy armoured cars, frigates and jet bombers, the police will still complain. It is like the biblical education of all waters flowing into the sea and the sea is never full. Every fool knows that the waters flowed back to where it came from. And when the *boys* are either not paid on time or not paid at all, the *ogas* know those who carry away the bags into which the funds flowed. Scores of Lubaba parallels have happened and the police was not disbanded. If we cannot do without them, we must accommodate the associated jeopardies. They function with hair raising precision only at ceremonies and the timely ceremony of the Fair Treatment For Women Programme has again obscured the slipshodness of a group seen by other arms of the security service as a national disgrace.

*　　　　*　　　　*

"Ex-husband, ex-wife, former home, divorce, separation, *babandagbe*, *iyandagbe*, are words we dread and fear when we were young," Inspector General of Police, Okoh Fatunlah, opened his speech on behalf of Mr. President, General Baguludu at the symposium fully attended by women delegates from all states of the federation.

The high table was actually high. Only the high-ups lined it from one end to the other. It was the fourth time the chairperson of the Fair Treatment for Women Programme (*FTWP*), Mrs. Ruth Baguludu, would bring together, women delegates of not less than one hundred from each of the states of the federation, spotting same local batik uniform with a spare, all given free. Mrs. Baguludu turned frequently from side to side and, at each turning, the gold earring on her sizeable lobe which reached to her shoulders dazzled every eye. Except for the three men on the eleven-sitter high table, all necks carry chains with heavy pendants and least a ring. Since the treatment must be fair, who dare talk?

Highly literate and gifted women who served as resource persons and contributors with scholastic presentations, demonstrating, depth in their various fields came in informal attires. They held their heads high above the shoulders with no rings bridging the gap, but in this category also, the eyewares were various. The eyewares matched the uniforms and headgears and for every five delegates, four appeared in eyewares. They are part of the dressing and not vision aids as originally conceived. Women were there, and across the hall were a parade of national monumental women. Women in their thirties, with springy bodies bouncing from place to place.

Those in their forties, with fluffy and maturely luscious bodies, who take everything, including the normal dosage, with confidence. And the above fifties who move their flabby remnants with caution. They are the categories who do it sparingly because they wish to live and see their grand children. Women were there, including those who study and know their men as reflected in their mien and views on the topic of the symposium. The *IGP* later resumed his speech after concluding his survey of the women deep in his mind. With watering mouth and pulsating body, he was already at the edge of the grave and needed only a shove to tumble over. Thank God, his wife was there.

"Those words came those days but they came rarely. Today the most boldly written word in the dictionary of matrimony is divorce. Why? The answer is that today's couples no longer want love, they want romance and romance are sweet nothings while love is a daily sweet dosage given more by the woman to keep the home going. Before now, marriage meant having someone you can grow old with, but today marriage is seen as providing someone on whose back you can ride to power. Have a good job, buy a car, build a house, have good savings and thereafter break the golden cord of marriage since you can now live alone. In those days, matrimony was what we see our fathers and mothers do enviously in their illiterate stature; enduring and keeping nothing back and leaving no room for mistrust.

"Today, matrimony is what we learn from movies and newspaper pages, acted and written by the age peers of our last child. There is no arguing the fact that today, matrimony is no longer a wedlock, and if a wedlock is not a padlock, men and women will fuck and sleep around, quarrel ceaselessly, curse, nag, abuse, tell lies and hide their bodies from each other. All these are done in the presence of grown-up children. What a damage we do to our homes and later run back to the churches to rebuke Satan..."

"Shame on Satan," the women chorused as they often do in public.

"To be realistic and truthful, most of the matrimonial disorders are caused by women. The beginning of a break in the home is when the woman is always wanting, never satisfied, ceaselessly complaining and with few thousands in her accounts, becoming unruly and disrespectful to the husband. Every husband needs all the honour at home." Mr Fatunlah paused a little to direct attention to his wife who was the master of ceremony for the occasion. A brilliant lawyer and mother of three boys, she is seen as a humble woman and highly respected in the Police Officers Wives Association, inspite of the known escapades of her husband.

"I tell my wife all the time that her education will be nothing if she got lost in the euphoria of success, because she will end up equally lost, lonely and unsuccessful. This is a situation most women apprehensively make too many mistakes in trying to avoid, and into which they most often fall because of the inability to manage success. No man marries his enemy and, since women live longer than men, what you should do is to banish all fears of *'what happens to me later'*. This fear and that of *'the other imaginary woman,'* accounts for most mistakes made by women and unto which broken homes are tied.

"The wolf husband, the chain-smoking addict, the ruthless woman-basher and the incurable liars highly talented in craftiness and artfulness abound. But if he is the dog, do not attempt to be the dogcatcher. Look for someone to catch the dog, and in this case, God Almighty, the author and finisher of our faith. With these steps which I hope you will seriously consider during this symposium, the issue of hoodlums, miscreants, armed robbers, rapists, whores and pen robbers will reduce. The cells are over-crowded and to continue to keep our young ones in the cell is to cage our future.

"Most of you women dismantle your homes on the excuse that you suffered much for a man. But you do not know when your suffering will be enough, only God knows when you suffer enough. The best thing to do all the time is to take your flesh captive and know that your *yanga* must end the day you are married. You must realise that when a man fights to have something, in this case a woman, he will strive and fight to keep it. The woman is more than she knows herself to be."

As the national anthem sounded off to close the opening ceremony, the Head of Department for Gender Studies, Lapas University, Dr (Mrs) Helen Nwosu, put forward her hand to the IGP who was stepping out of the hall.

"Good speech, IGP; but too much on women's inadequacies," she remarked after introducing herself.

"Sorry Doctor, I merely read the speech of the C-in-C the number one husband and I share his views."

"Yes, they are alright. We tell our students these days, in view of the growing rate of divorce, that they have rights but that marriage is a battle of words and will; and that the man's will, not the woman's words, must prevail. If they decide to marry, they must constantly allow the words of their husbands to break them down because of the children and the future of society." Dr Nwosu sounded impressively knowledgeable in home matters.

"Good. And if that is part of the curriculum for gender studies, then the future is bright," the IGP gladly added.

"Oh yes, it is. In fact, we told them too in a recent seminar like this one for working class ladies, that peer influences have crept into, and dismantled most marriages with beautiful and enviable foundations. We urged them to know that, besides them and their husbands, any other person is an intruder. Women keep their family more than men keep theirs. We secretly shower them with what we cannot give to our in-laws where we have our futures. By that process, most of our families have dismantled the homes of their daughters by encouraging unfaithful gifts, social status presentations and financial rewards. We women must be careful of this nature of family influences. They must uproot them and marry their homes, and their children for the man who love them, is their future. They must make themselves reachable by their husbands to enable them to be teachable. Women must marry their homes."

"We men know that the ways to our heart is the stomach and the way to the heart of our women is flowery and sentimental words to educate and inform. Today's woman must endeavour to listen to what will make the children better leaders of tomorrow. They must be as gentle as a dove. I am happy my wife listens to me and she knows me quite well and my children are happy." He turned around almost full cycle before he located his wife in the sea of permed, braided, low-cut and damask-geared heads.

"Good, a woman must appreciate her husband, share his moments and not that of her friends, sisters and bosses. She must share his passion and actualise, daily, his likes and not the condemnation of people about him. Those who make such condemnations are far and she is the only one very close to him who can observe correctly. I must say, Doctor, that sixty percent of those in our cells are products of broken homes. What went wrong in the kitchen and the dining is causing stooling in the bedrooms. We are appealing to women participating in this symposium to take the message back to the states, local governments and villages."

Trust them. They did just that, but the devil still roared as they join in the jostle for contracts that abound in Amuta, leaving the comfort of their homes and their attendant duty to the children who must run the capital in the future. It is not funny at all. One of them once moved near the defence headquarters and, seeing a multitude in the blazing sun, she demanded to know why any woman must sun herself dry to see an army officer to sell same body.

She was told the women were struggling with their male counterparts for contract. She re-applied her powder, joined the queue and, few days later when she had been properly used to the facilities at the guest house of the colonel, she received a local purchase order of over thirty million naira to supply biros and file jackets. She was properly tasted and circulated.

Six months later, her husband lost her to the red necks, rendering seven children motherless in a matrimony they grew to know, love and believed-in for a great future.

order eight, rule eight

"...no state is ever clean. Many hands have been soiled"

The Mercedes Benz limo sped too rapidly from the airport to the villa at Amuta, such that many immediately knew that the occupants were special guests of a kind. There was no reason for any government to put eight limos and seven other protocol cars on an endless convoy for just eight human rights delegates from different developed countries, merely wishing to verify claims of human rights abuses and dimming prospects for democracy in the country. The visit was occasioned by representations made by a coalition of four human rights groups.

The distance from the airport was not much, but the drive round town was quite a stress, and the arrangement was to allow individual work-up on the visitors by the state security guides. The visitors expected it but not in that form and the tremendous resources committed to its actualisation.

"I must say that I am quite impressed by the extent and the great details into which your government went, your excellency, to make us comfortable in this assignment we have set for ourselves," Peter Scott, the leader of the delegation told President Baguludu at a meeting later in the day.

"Within the next few days, Sir, my colleagues are hopeful that our visit would have begun to record the success this delegation is here for. For now, we do no talking, just seeing and assessing. The reports in the international press are not too encouraging. The feelers from your own nationals abroad are equally glib, indicating largely that you do too many things wrongly and without care. Anyway, we are on ground and we are testing to see if the load is too heavy for the land or if the soil itself is bad soil."

There was actually nothing to say, but much to assess: and to properly assess, however, is the litmus test. It was not the first time that a delegation of a similar mission would be coming to assess the genuineness of a military regime.

A former president of the world's most matured democracy came soon after the Baguludu junta came to power. He had a tour. At least sixteen of the twenty airports in the country saw the screeching and take off of the presidential jet tyres. What made the rounds later were talks and insinuations that the tour was part of a world health body's plan to eradicate guinea-worm in Africa.

"This country, by available assessments, is the worst and greatest victim, and eradication must begin from here. If this government can successfully eradicate guinea-worm from the waters, then all other things shall be added unto it," he was quoted as saying on his way out of the country. If the Bible asked you to seek first the kingdom of God and its glory, for other things to be added thereafter, then, one can also preach the gospel medically.

If late Kwame Nkrumah was too politically recalcitrant when he urged his people to fiercely fight colonialism thereby seeking first, political freedom (democracy), to enable the rectification of poverty, squalor and diseases, including guinea-worms, why must ours start with guinea-worm eradication and not political emancipation? The visit of the Scott delegation was described by Bishop Joshua Lubaba as: 'a race with the shadows by a man who has rubbed himself deep into khaki clad clowns.' President Baguludu however saw the present visit as an apple of a different sore requiring a new approach.

"Please move round and be free to ask questions. My administration is tenacious about our promise to make this government the last military regime in this country. If we rush out, we will again make the succeeding civilian administration an interregnum. No! We can't do that! No. We won't rush out. This regime stands for something corrective and we will not fall for anything dishonourable.

"The problem is that everyone here is talented in relentless devilish political dexterity. Since we came to power, we have put down two coup attempts so that the life of this administration, which is a continuation of military rule by understanding, will not be extended. Even with our genuine intention to go as soon as it is convenient, we receive applications daily for the positions of ministers, special advisers and chairmen of parastatals. They don't want us to go, but go we will. How is your country...."? General Baguludu suddenly changed the course of discussion, to the amazement of the leader of the delegation.

"Fine. You mean my president? Fine."

"No! Your country in view of the current worldwide recession?" he was still clinging to the new course.

"Well, your excellency, I think we are alright. However, only the secretary for commerce is in position to give an accurate assessment of the situation. A non-governmental organization like ours, performing a non-governmental duty abroad, is in no position to make sensitive government policy pronouncements." Mr. Scott wraps up everything before the delegation retired to their hotel.

*   *   *

Dr. Amba Zuma, the Minister of Information, was again ideologically mouthy as he opened a page of another lecture series when the delegation visited him the next day in his office. As the ENG camera rolled away images of mouthful laughter and firm hand-shakes, Dr. Zuma opened his lengthy tirade. He must do his job.

"Mr. Scott, you are welcome to my office and please accept felicitations for all members of your delegation. Mr. Scott, you will soon discover that no one here is in government to scuttle anyone.

"The mood in this office is the mood nationwide. We sell happiness and no one is making life difficult for the other. This is not a government with a tendency to feign deafness when people express their views. It is the nature of man to want to be rebellious and quarrelsome especially with an administration giving him the limitless access to opportunities for a life more abundant. It is only when that opportunity eludes him that he realises the folly he had been led into by the distant foreign press. They always portray us as never doing enough. The war in the horn, is for example, raking-in money through increase in crude oil prices. This we are using to build roads. They are all over the place and no *panlogo* on our roads again, even when it is known that we have the largest network in Africa.

"Ours is an emerging power, and aspirants to the largesse of government will want a hand-over as swift as possible. But little do they know that government programmes cannot be implemented overnight. Even in your country, Mr. Scott, you are still developing. The opposition will talk but the government reacts minimally to such criticisms. The United Nations was created to prevent the scourge of war, yet wars still rage all over the world. Signatories to the UN Charter are selling arms to sustain just and unjust wars on the fields, while engaging the world body in complex conferences and administrative details. They rake in blood money into their treasuries in defiance of morality in order to live on the lips of men.

"Prisons are meant to reform criminals and minimise criminal tendencies, but the prisons are built and expanded daily to suggest the growing rate of crime. Then, why must anyone lose sleep about any government in power, which, in any event, is transient? I have not seen any everlasting or life government other than the government of God; the incumbent of all incumbents. Life presidents are never for life. Time usually consumed them and they are overtaken by death. The Baguludu administration will follow the same course, that is, consigned into the storehouse of fame rather than the dustbin of history. This I know. One day we will become history."

Dr. Zuma surveyed the rapt attention in the room, reclined his chair and continued. "In the course of your visit, talk to some politicians if you can find any. They are all over the federal capital, looking for appointments and contracts from a junta they denounce in the papers but into which they are closely fused, to the extent that they sometimes dictate the direction for some government policies. Discover their seriousness, gauge their commitment to reconciliation and understanding, imagine their vision for a nation as greatly blessed as ours, then make up your minds. All we are to do is to logistically support you, to ensure that your movements, accommodation and leisure in the course of this assignment are without much labour. And this we will do, even at the cost of the expected ingratitude of compensating us with a negative report.

"This administration will not mind any report published, because we know that you know that we are on the right course to national progress. Everyone can see that! Even the human rights group which invited you can see this."

Indeed, everyone saw the gestures, especially the visiting fact-finding team whose dinner was disturbed by the broadcast at 7 p.m. that evening by the president,

General Ramos Baguludu. He announced a four-year timetable for transition to civil rule.

Hot, fresh and smoking rumour, as well as the steady stream of speculations, soon became real. The junta announced a four-year transition programme, a staggered agenda that looked unending. First, a national headcount to determine an accurate census. The last one, which was described as the least disputable, may no longer be valid since the junta claimed that it contained some quarrelsome flaws capable of setting off ethnic discontent and protests, if used. This is to be followed by a compilation of a register of voters for the delimitation of wards, constituencies and senatorial districts. Only after these would the politicians not included in a proscription list yet to be released, be allowed to form political associations, with a view to contesting elections.

Election to the houses of assembly in the states and gubernatorial elections will hold in the second year of the transition programme. This will mean an overlapping of a military and civilian administration, the military in control at the centre, while politicians take charge in the states and local governments on a non-party basis. The final election to the senate and the House of Representatives and the election of the president will cap the transition program...

"Mr. Scot, you remember I told you we are on course," Dr. Zuma sang gleefully on the telephone to score a point with the leader of delegation.

"Oh! Honourable minister, but you didn't let that out to me in the morning. Why?" Scot demanded.

"Yes, the *C-in-C* decided on the broadcast very late. Tomorrow is Human Rights Day and General Baguludu decided to give the goodies to commemorate the day as a military government with the interest of the people at heart? Tell your governments at home that this is not a junta. It is not a regime. It is a properly constituted administration. We are human all over, not only in the face."

"Oh, Dr. Zuma. Leave that to us. We recognise what we are seeing. We have souls and feelings too. We can think. Leave our judgements to us! We are not working for any government. This is an *NGO* affair, though our government gave the backing."

"O.K, Mr. Scott, we are seriously privatising now to divest government of investments in some areas better run by private hands. The *C-in-C* is of the view that one of our five-star hotels could be good for your participation. There is also this allocation of industrial estate plots at the new federal capital. I am to secure allocation papers for you if you wish and..."

"Oh! You are wonderful. You are actually transiting. But sorry, the anti-corruption act in my country forbids me from accepting any gift worth more than twenty dollars. Anything above this is a donation to the state and you can make such generous donation through our embassy. The Inspector General is on my cellular line. We are meeting him tomorrow. Sorry!..."

"Hello! Hello!!....." Scot's phone went mute, not necessarily talking to any inspector general.

*   *   *

"Is that the way a military administration discharges the duty of state, by appropriating scarce resources recklessly while the masses suffer?" he opened the discussion with the leader of the National Student's Association. Representatives of the association came to testify before the team in one of the open sessions organised for the human rights team. The student leader had suddenly opened an area the team was sceptical in touching, the area of financial accountability in government.

"The military is a spender in government, and not a saver. University education has died, college education is forgotten and primary education is no more. The collapsed walls of the classrooms which prepared them for the uniform they now use to steal public funds are testimonies. The uniform in this country is a pleasure wear and not a combat outfit. This is a country that parades the highest number of generals in the continent, complete with shining gold necklaces and rings on all fingers procured from Harrods. Although, I am yet to see an ideal state without a soiled hand..."

"Do you think they really looted the treasury?"

"Ostentation is running riot everywhere. In their cars, in their homes, on their children; and you will, at a glance, perceive the limitless acquisitive instincts in them. No federal scholarship has been awarded in the last three years. No state government bursaries have been given. What we have, rather, are bullets to kill and maim hungry students when they protest the falling and failing standard of education which is putting the life of our future generation into jeopardy. Education is in crisis and the only alternative for growth is democracy. The future, as they see it, is in our petroleum which they merchandise daily, with their immediate family, and they don't invest the proceeds in the education of our children. They pretend not to be aware that these neglected children will be the future geologists and politicians."

"The regime has announced a transition programme." Mr. Scott interrupted him.

"They are merely transiting into their pockets. Why do they need four years to transit to the barracks? This is a confirmation of a hidden agenda and nothing more. Four years is the life of a normal government if they do not wish to turn their ranks into crowns and their offices into palaces. It is very unrealistic and too long to execute a programme of transition. They are here again holding us by the throat. We students do not take them seriously anymore."

And indeed they were already holding the nation by the throat as the report of the Scott Delegation glaringly displayed too much favour for the military government, which responded with series of broadcasts and statements to amend or restructure the transition agenda following what they saw as an acquittal.

*   *   *

"*Allah Kua!* We are moving out!" the chief of naval staff told journalists as he slipped into his *staff car* after commissioning the latest frigate in the naval fleet at the Western Naval Command Headquarters in Lapas.

"The *C-in-C* is a political selection by the military and I cannot speak for him, but all I know is that the service chiefs have been given their orders to keep our boys assured that we are moving to the barracks anytime from now."

"But the transition programme keeps changing, Sir, suggesting that the four-year programme is constantly being..."

"You journalists speculate too much. The government has set out a programme of action. The government is not perfect and can make mistakes. We are keeping faith with the programme and correcting the inherent mistakes as we go along. You can see how the two fact-finding teams commended our genuine commitment to an emerging and highly articulated democratic process. Your paper reported the findings of the Scott Delegation less than six months ago. Isn't it? Four months from now, the local government and governorship elections will hold. Just wait and see."

"Yes, Sir. But there are rumours that the Scot team was also bought over with substantial gratifications which it refused initially, but later fell flat for it."

"Ask Mr. Scott about that. This administration is lucky to always find people to buy over. We will soon come and buy over the managing director of your newspaper to serve as special adviser on '*buy-overs.*' All I know is that, barring unforeseen circumstances, the four-year transition stays. We will hand over. What is four years in any event? A bright student admitted for medicine stays there for five years, with two additional years for housemanship and national service. He gets out to be a saver of souls and an asset to the nation. Let us see ourselves as students studying political science for the next four years. The most important thing is to pass and be qualified, to give the right political leadership. God forbid another military take-over. Already, one year is almost gone out of four. We should be talking about the elections now and not the programme.

"Already, we have our orders to ensure that all is calm in our barracks and to report unusual movements of men and ordinance appropriately. All service chiefs will do this to any extent that military logistics allow. But don't tempt our boys with money. You melt and obey all orders when we point our nozzles and bayonets at you. We equally melt and become fretful when you offer millions to us to do an odd job. We are all criminals in a lone cell. We all need counseling, new deliverance and fresh anointing."

"But the millions are nothing to soldiers in this country, Sir. It appears that making millions is part of their commission and with the coming elections, it is sure that millions will disappear again. Who dare ask you?"

"Thank you. But the day I see a million naira, I will faint!" the press boys roared in ceaseless laughter as the blue *staff car* flaps away the navy flag, with a two-star general screen-printed emblem, preceded by two outriders in a deafening wail.

"If my boss will faint, I will rapture," the naval director of information, Captain Tiwa Leti brought back the discussion as they walked away for a tour of the frigate.

It was the latest frigate in the naval fleet with an astonishing speed for her weight of 30,500 tones. It was fitted with modern weapons and a capacity for four hundred sailors.

"Besides, there are five 22-inch guns..." Captain Leti was going into specifics. "...Four Vulcan bombers and two sea- king attack helicopters can take off and land on board. The helicopters are equipped with night vision devices to make the strafing of enemy lines possible with bewildering accuracy and rapid delivery.

"This is a deadly ship with computer assisted torpedoes capable of streaking across waves undetected. She is also fitted with facilities to launch *Milan* and *exocet* missiles with *tandem* warheads. Besides..."

"I think I will be the first to faint with these scaring details," the same reporter opened the issue again.

"But you haven't seen any millions yet?" Captain Leti offered a relief.

"Yes. But I am face-to-face with the deadly nature of what millions can buy to reduce man to nothing. Man, this is where all the monies go." The laughter was brief and the captain continued his explanation.

"Honestly, I must add that these awesome equipments are not for comic, but deadly wars. We also have the ability to sweep mines and her armoury is a glittering array of sager and stinger missiles, mortar shells, grenades, small arms and ammunition.

"We have half a dozen rafts for swamp and beach landing. You may be right that this is where the monies go, not uniforms. In fact, we now buy uniform by ourselves if you don't want to look shabby. Not even the traditional '*housewives*' as we know it in the military now come easy. We must be combat ready and be able to deter any aggression. Everyone knows this but they prefer that we are caught pants-down when aggression rears."

"This is impressive." The National Television editor remarked.

"Yes. Money in the military is cash-and-spend, not cash-and-keep. Our salary is what we have. No '*egunje.*' No officer can buy a frigate, a jaguar jet, an attack helicopter or an armoured personnel carrier. The ministry of defence is responsible. You buy and we operate. How you buy, we don't know. We arm for war. We don't war for arm. No!"

"But you maintain them with the millions." The reporter who started it all opened up again.

"We have a culture of maintenance. That's all I know. Like my boss, I have never seen a million physically. The day I come across one, I will definitely rapture." The laughter came off again and much of it, this time, was light hearted.

Opinions were freely expressed at the naval mess later where the reporters were treated to drinks. *The News* reporter sounded more explicit:

"I think it was a former prime minister who once said that the navy is nothing but rum, lash and sodomy. I tend to believe. I was cautioned that the golden rule in a naval mess is to know when to stop. If you rum ceaselessly, you will rumble later and I need a good *'intro'*."

They were good words spoken in due season with a prophetic underlay. Few kilometres away, rumblings at the famous *Uleye* barracks later became too hot to handle.

Ever since the transition programme was announced, some set of army officers have felt short changed. They have considered the role-call to honour moving gradually in their favour aborted especially with the just concluded arrangements for local government and governorship elections which brought no pandemonium and chaos as expected. The method to be used to elect candidates who cared to apply on non-party basis, has not been bedevilled with any acrimony. This was unbelievable. No one thought it was going to work and for this, the restless group have learnt to change their responses to emergencies. They closely watch every move of government with a view to catching-in on any little distress situation as an opportunity for action to disturb the elections. What does it matter putting their lives on the line? Afterall, we must constantly find someone to hate so that we can love others. If the elections do not hold, it would be minus to a few, but a plus to many whose course they chose to champion, as usual, unsolicited.

order nine, rule nine

"...coups and executions; first and second taps of funeral drums
for several brilliant ones."

"*Who ask you to open gate to ordinance depot? Eh! Who
order you?*" the *RSM* raged at the captain.

"*You want to take over government again, eh? So, this
government is not good enough. You want to be governor
and chop money too? Who be Major Suba Gash self?*"

Captain Dan Bala was mute. The coup was already
on, and he must learn to keep his mouth shut; else, he
would be expressly assisting to put down the putsch
while the battle was still raging at the broadcasting
house. The pendulum could swing to any side. He was
unlucky to be the first to be overpowered while trying
to send re-enforcement to the putschists.

The war room at the defence headquarters was
reeling out orders to the assault group at the presidential
villa via radio communication. Troops movement in
santana jeeps was all over Amuta. President Baguludu's
Rocky villa had been attacked at exactly 5.30 a.m. with
two armoured personnel carriers and ten men who
blasted their way into the fortress. The roof of the villa
was ripped-off in the violent exchange of fire which
scuttled the *ADC* and the president out of bed. The
immediate directives were specific: to order the ordinance
depot shut thereby preventing a replenishment of armour.

Arrest the duty officer, call out the elite Special Protection Group, *SPG*, to counter the move by storming the national station at all material, civil and military costs; and to stop further announcements of the coup. Lapas was far away, but military logistics respect no distance, especially with the Lapas Garrison as the most potent arm of the composite *2nd Division* in the former capital.

The coup announcements were actually awry and more damaging than the putsch itself. It was the first time *vox pops* were used to convince the docile *bloody civilians* that people were already accepting the putschists even when they were yet to put out the ruling junta and dislodge the commander-in-chief at the *Rocky Villa*.

Students, traders, civil servants, businessmen and ragtags who feigned diplomats, all went on air claiming to be interviewed from different locations in the country. The game was perfect and must have been learnt from experienced plotters, thereby confirming the military as conspirators in high treason; a group of expendable national actors seriously unqualified to move near power because of their terrifying talents. The coup leader, Major T. S. Gash, was a former state governor and a good boy of Brigadier Yom Yizor, recently removed as Minister of Defence.

The quarter-hourly broadcast was incisively indicting of the regime the putschists tried to discredit and push out. "... We have so far been subjected to a steady deterioration in our standard of living and intolerable suffering by the ordinary man. Now, the suffering has reached unprecedented heights.

"Prices of goods and equipment have risen higher, scarcity of commodities has increased, hospitals still remain consulting centres while educational institutions are on the brink of total collapse. The *Baguludu Junta* has further fragmented us, such that we can no longer talk of a sound, united and stable nation. You have heard the views of a cross-section. They include those who were buying a beetle car for ₦7,600.00, but now had to pay ₦150,000.00 for a fairly used. The housewife who was buying a bag of rice for ₦150.00 but who must now take a salary advances to buy same bag for ₦5,000.00. We have been thrown from economic wilderness to economic doldrums, and impediments are daily introduced to the ability of politicians to lead. You will then know that the out-going administration of General Baguludu was a great leap backward..."

As usual, the nation stood still again. No movements except in the direction of putting down the new uprising. The old and the emerging leapers had no reason to leap at all. Baguludu had no reason to stay in government and Gash had no excuse also to want to rule. The backward leapers leapt into a hallway of disgrace. Price comparison and the use of *vox pop* did not work. Baguludu was back in power in less than six hours. Thanks to the daring efforts of Colonel Ade Michael who stormed the national station, and he lost his life in the process. After arresting Major Suba Gash at the radio station, he had forcefully opened the door to *Studio 2* to ensure complete retrieval of all the tapes from the Ampex machines. The sergeant detailed to ensure smooth transmission of the coup broadcast identified him as an enemy and promptly opened fire. He gunned him down with two other soldiers before he was put out, himself, along with the lady continuity announcer who ran into the line of fire in panic. The studio manager was also fatally wounded.

That was the news that travelled most widely as many argued that, if Colonel Ade Michael actually put down the coup, his broadcast was the one expected and not that of his second-in-command. The information given at his unit was that he was put out in the uprising, which was the bloodiest so far in the nation's coup history. The news reached his wife soonest inspite of attempts to conceal it and use officers to break it later.

"Where is *Oga*?" Mrs Michael shouted at the quarter guards, almost falling as she staggered out of the Honda Prelude car to confirm the rumour at the office of the military secretary. She had forcefully moved out of the barracks and against all persuations to reach the office. The drive down was too absent minded and she saw none of the military checkpoints on her way.

"*Sorry, Madam. Oga no dey here!*"

"Where is he? Where?"

"No idea, Madam. I saw only his body, not him, on the way to the hospital!"

"Hospi... Boorrrdy!" and she was receding, holding tightly to the corporal's shirt.

"*Sorry, Madam! Oga no dey here! Ah, Corporal call O.C oh! Madam don collapse o! This army work self! Call O.C! Call O.C!*"

As the long drawn day struck 4.30 p.m., General Baguludu appeared at the press centre of the Presidential Villa to address a world press conference. Dressed in full battle gear with jackboot and jungle hat, he caught the picture of an embattled soldier just escaping from an enemy territory with gasps. His smile had disappeared. The chief of army staff and the head of army intelligence bordered him off at both sides in similar camouflage outfits.

"This conference is necessary to principally assure the nation and the international community that all is well. I am still in charge here. The insurrection, which took place early today by a group of disgruntled men, has been put under control. This administration is intact and our programme of transition is on course. The short broadcast to the nation at 4 p.m. said everything. We are on course and no setback at all. Thank you for co-operating. I will answer your questions." Fright was still visible in him.

"But, Sir, did the plot shake your government?" *The Mirror* reporter was quick to ask.

"Well, yes. Just like any *coup d'état*. You never can tell what they have up their sleeves until they finish, or are prevented from rounding off."

"What about the plotters, Sir?"

"Those boys were deadly animals with pure criminal mentalities. Major Gash himself was arrested at the national station. In all, twenty men, including six officers, have so far been arrested. The military intelligence is still working. There may be more, by direct involvement or complicity. They will face a military court martial as soon as possible. We were startled, but only in view of the political programme lay-out. We would have gone back a full cycle, had they succeeded. Those boys were real mad."

"You were a putschist yourself and you had a taste of the action from the other side this time," *The Mirror* reporter chipped in again.

"Yes, and it is permitted. Only a failure is criminal and punishable. I didn't fail. They failed. Putschists and mutineers are two of a kind, and it is success that matters. But if you fail, I am sorry."

"Don't you think that their excuses are credible?"

"I don't know. They can make their case to the court martial. They will be given a fair trial."

"Any insight into the lives lost, Sir?"

"The least permissible under such circumstances. But principally we lost a high-ranking officer in the assault on the Radio House. He will be buried with full military honours tomorrow. Generally, gentlemen of the press, I have to thank my service chiefs who mustered all resources to ensure that our programme of handing-over was not derailed. Those boys were too good in military tactics. *Haba!* Their shellings were too accurate to targets, and with their rifles they shot precisely. This is the stuff of which our boys are made. We treat every situation as a serious war situation, no matter what level of armament is involved. That's the way we were trained and the exact reason why we try to prevent bloody coups if it is possible. The loss of one fine officer and some boys is painful, especially when it is a senseless coup. We must try to prevent coups. We must try. Nothing will deter us from the programme laid out. Already, the election of governors on non-party basis is coming up very soon. It must hold."

The trial of the putchists was handled and concluded with dispatch. Whatever happened to the boys, a patient nation was thinking, was their own lookout since it was their commission to kill or be killed. The only regret was that very fine officers were either killed, maimed, retired or declared *AWOL* after fleeing from arrest, trial and conviction for their role in a coup that served the morbid ambition of a few national ingrates.

The coup finally yielded twenty-eight arrests including one Major John Odele, a brilliant officer from the Airborne Brigade in Bagama, Plamana State. He was condemned to death for concealment of treason. His mitigation of sentence on the national news was too harrowing and chilling.

"My Lord," he told Brigadier Paul Waris, Chief Marshal of the military court, "I have very little to say if the terms of my commission gave no alternative to a frame-up. Twice I have been implicated in coups, and twice the operators of a system that gave me ceaseless horror as a serving officer, have stabbed me at the back. I was serving in Kabari where I learnt of a coup attempt, which I promptly reported to my brigade commander, Lt. Col. Ukah. I was scolded and locked up only to be released the third day to find him, a key figure in the coup, announced as governor. I was then posted to Lishi where, few months later, I got wind of another coup. Again I promptly reported to my *GOC* and that was the rudest shock of my life. I was flown out in handcuffs and leg-chains and put into confinement at the maximum prison in Lapas. Three weeks later, the gate of my cell was opened and I discovered that my boss was the new head of state, the present commander-in-chief, General Baguludu.

"For this coup, I heard it ordinarily as a rumour at the Tombola Night and found it difficult to report again. First, I haven't enough evidence like I had in the first two instances; and also, the fear of being locked up again was there.

"But Sir, let me add that it is equally an irony of history that you, who read out my commission at the academy, recommended me for two overseas training courses and wrote briefs for my latest promotion to the rank of a Major, are the same person that is presiding over the termination of my life. May your Lordship be pleased!"

The mitigation was the only item allowed to run its full length after the chief of army staff had briefly appeared, reading from a prepared speech to inform a bewildered nation that in all, twenty eight officers and men were tried. Sixteen were found guilty of high treason, five were jailed and seven discharged and acquitted. The execution of the sixteen found guilty of high treason was carried out early this morning after confirmation by the Revolutionary State Council. They include the former Defence Minister, Brigadier Yom Yizor and a former State Governor, Major T. S. Gash...

Tears flowed freely in most homes as another darkness enveloped the nation. Another set of brilliant men sacrificed to sustain the ambition of a few in khaki.

Sixteen more men dispatched to the great beyond in the shameless cleavage by a few who would now continue to major in a calling that is entirely outside and distant from their service mandate. Perhaps, the staring question is that, if great empires had been plucking their children at prime, then who would have been those heroes we daily read about in the history books? Alexander the Great, son of Philip of Macedon, provided leadership for the great nation-state of Greece at the age of twenty-two. If he had been dispatched early in life, how would he have led the Grecian Army to conquer the then known world including Alexandria that was named after him. If the Mongol warlord, Genghis Khan, had been speared at his prime, he could not have had the opportunity to use his Asian Hordes to conquer the entire vast land stretching out thousands of kilometres from his native land, Mongolia.

If Winston Churchill, George Washington and others were executed early in life because of the morbid ambition of a few, then their writings, forever bringing credence and honour to their countries and knowledge to humanity, would have gone with them to the graves. This is the genuine fear, the concern and the bane about these blood thirsty military boy. If not cast off by practical action, they would persist and draw the nation back many decades, thereby stalling development. The military has no mandate to waste the lives it was established to protect.

The military junta itself knew. And three months after the executions, the army headquarters in Lapas opened its doors to the widow of one of the convicted putschists.

"Morning, Madam, and how are the children?" Colonel Tonye, the defence spokesman opened up.

"Fine Sir, and God is in control in our home. We lost our breadwinner but God is the ultimate breadwinner."

"We just want you to fill this form for any of your sons between age ten and twelve, and submit immediately."

"Sorry, Sir. For what purpose?" she demanded explanation to such a gesture to the wife of an executed treasonable felon, late Major John Odele.

"Free training at the military school, Madam for the child. Good leadership training and education from child-hood."

"Sorry, Sir. I don't want any of my children to grow up in a culture soaked in conspiracy and national condemnation. I have four fatherless boys on my hand. One of them in the military cannot fill the gap left by their father. I am sorry, Sir. No military life for any of them. I am sorry, Sir." Mrs. Odele muttered back, already in tears. What an opportunity! Since the tears came, the announcement of the shocker will not induce blood, only tears. But the three rednecks performing the odd duty were wrong.

"Madam, this gesture is from the Revolutionary State Council. One of your children has been given automatic scholarship to pursue a carrier in any of the forces. Besides, your husband's salary and rank have been restored and this will be paid in full for life to his next of kin, which is you. A discreet investigation has shown that your husband, our very fine officer, Major John Odele, was executed in error and..."

"What did you say? My husband executed in er...r..." She fainted. The army doctor on stand-by tirelessly worked to no avail.

And the woman died! Another family wasted in military adventurism and for the ambition of a few. Such were some of the ways lives were wasted and families dispossessed of their breadwinners. Because of the hurried and pancake approach to decision-making involving lives, countless of such lives were sent on *'leave'* to enable others to bloom and flourish in stolen wealth and make a clique feast of *cakes* baked for all. They wished to be spoken about, and with power and money in their closet, they became deaf when people talked reason. The military made life a general drama of pain, sorrow and despair while happiness and hope, the essence of life, became nightmares and occasional episodes.

Everyone woke up daily to discover that life was dirty, brutish and worthless, as those who were not the architects of life sniff it out at will. We paid the price, as Dr Zuma predicted during the argument at the university staff club before he became information minister in the junta of General Baguludu and sold his conscience for a plate of porridge.

Such were the biology of men who served under Baguludu. Men who called shots at home and at press conferences but became lilies in office and cabinet meetings. They kept their heads very deep in water to be able to keep their food on table and they paint Baguludu style as holistic by every standard. As the election of governors and assembly members commenced without parties, they were used to convince the people to move ahead with the alien political approach. The human rights activists displayed their usual thoughtful restlessness while politicians who were sceptical of his plans, stayed off and cried on newspaper pages regularly.

In spite of this, governors were still handpicked and voters guided to line-up behind posters that showed nothing about any contestant and their plans, but their colourful pictures. Baguludu's choices moved into the government houses and immediately went to the work of preparing the people for an agenda, hidden to all, but daily fine-tuned by the Baguludu brigade.

order ten, rule ten

"... too rich to be poor and to beg forgiveness."

The queue was long, with automobiles stretching far to a kilometre. The rancour was unending, each trying to seize the nozzle from the attendant and fill up before the other. Not less than a quarter of an hour is needed to fill a tank as arguments, explanations, wailings, political lectures and unnecessary technical jargons criss-cross and compete for attention.

The confusion had been such for twenty days, following the strike action by tanker-drivers protesting the horsewhip approach in forcefully diverting consignments from the loading depots to military cantonments. The nation-wide strike was worsened by the arrest and detention of the national secretary who ordered it and who insisted in an interview, erroneously relayed by the national television network, that no driver must resume duties until he gave a counter directive through the same medium.

The suffering was tense and the hazards of securing a litre of gas too grave. *Pressure boys* carry aloof four litre cans by the roadside at prices high enough to feed an average family for a week. The nation's administrative machinery was grounded and the *S & T* engineers in the three arms of the military faced an uphill task, loading and discharging commandeered tankers to keep few essential services running. All sectors of the economy were affected and *Atibiri* road, the main artery out of Lapas, linking the city with other parts of the country as well as other major city roads, became football fields for children whose teachers could not get to school. Not less than ten houses and a score cars were razed by hoarders who operated a risky but highly thriving storage business. The *GAM* station at the new federal capital Amuta, sent shrills to the *Rocky Villa* when scufflers sprayed petrol on the over-heated pumping machine. The explosion was deafening and devastating. Four men lay dead and seven others were hospitalised for various degrees of burn. The crowd used the occasion to merchandise in group slander on the military about their bad decisions, squandermania, wrong priorities and other misadventures.

The independence anniversary was just a few days ahead and the jeopardy was to leave the security unsolved and deceitfully sermonise on life more abundant for the people, or stem the chaos and forgo a broadcast.

"The double jeopardy is surmountable." General Baguludu told his service chiefs and other members of the highest ruling body at an emergency meeting.

"The *C-in-C*, Sir, the situation is chaotic and it is nation-wide!" the naval chief painted the national gloom accurately.

"Yes, I know. But we must solve it. This is the work of our detractors, the politicians. The explosion at the refinery is nothing; the tanker drivers are the problem. The refinery is running again and security reports show that the strike was engineered by a prominent politician who is claiming that the new governors in the states are stooges manipulated there by the zero party strategy. He will fail. We have concluded that phase of the transition and no one will take us back," he paused to flip his brief to the next page.

"I equally have reports that the two hundred tankers ordered by the last administration are lying waste, but in perfect condition, at the works yard in Lapas. I have directed the transport minister to distribute them to all the states. By now, they should be running with drivers from the army. The situation is under control, let us talk about the broadcast, the anniversary broadcast." General Baguludu cut a posture of non-challance.

"The broadcast, Sir?"

"Yes, what about it, *IGP*?"

"I just think that if we have to do it at all, we must put a little flesh into it. Tell them what they want to hear, even if events will move in another direction. My boys are in town daily and people talk. *Sir, they talk o!* We move our units around frequently, but new units give same old reports. We cannot manage any violent reaction in addition to the chaos on ground. The civilians are staging a coup."

"*Wan-dar-ful!* And you are inspector-general? *Wan-dar-ful!* Gentlemen, let us discuss the broadcast briefly. I know his problem, his people and their fears. It is the impending consequence of their inability to use fifty-four men to prevent a script from leaking to the press from an ordinary clergy that they wished to hide. They now struggle desperately to use thoughts to thwart such fears," the head of state made a recall of the Bishop Lubaba incident with visible rage, and no serious business was conducted any longer. Whatever the speechwriter to the head of state had written for consideration at the meeting for anniversary broadcast especially on the program for transition and eligibility, was adopted hook, line and sinker, and it thoroughly bewildered the nation. It was a long list of disqualifying orders:

* "..........All politicians who occupied offices in the two republics are barred from participating in the next republic.

* All those convicted of offences by military tribunals, courts or internal commissions of inquiry are banned.

* All electoral commissioners, returning officers, and justices who handled past cases relating to electoral petitions and other matters are banned.

* Any candidate for the position of president must not be less than fifty years before the year of election.

* Civil servants wishing to participate in partisan politics must resign their appointments six months before elections are held.

* The race to form parties by the people is unhealthy. Consequently, all associations seeking registration are disbanded and members are to harmonize or align their proposed manifestos to the three political parties created by government.

"You must remember that our years of independence have been used to form varieties of parties that were ideologically bankrupt and operationally defective," he remarked in the broadcast.

"Three parties, the Leftist Party (LP), the Centralist Party (CP) and the Rightist Party (RP), are hereby created, and every politician is free to join any of the three, and the procedure for choosing the party chairman will be spelt out in the enabling decree to be promulgated. I must add here that our democratisation process began some months ago with the election of governors and local government chairmen on zero-party basis. All the governors are now free to join the parties of their choice. If the parties had come before the local and state elections, we would not have been anywhere. We did what we think was right and we owe no apologies to anyone. The centre is very important and no politician of dubious character must be allowed to move near the *Villa*. With honesty at the centre, the state and the local governments can be effectively monitored.

"I must add here also that, under a special ban are all retired military officers whose penchant and stock in trade is now to violently criticise the government they have diligently served immediately power slipped off their hands."

As expected, it was another bittersweet broadcast of new sets of orders. Sometimes, Baguludu's intentions are laudable. Sometimes, they contain so much excellence, far too rosy to be real. Analysts believed that his style of sledgehammer approach to situations very often put off the heat before it degenerates into a fire. He was a suffocation maniac that succeeded in grabbing the nation by the throat and the nation is perilously dangling under his hold.

"The head of state is a peripheral nonsense with medieval tirades that are manifestations of his weird thoughts and ideas." The chairman of the Lapas City

Council, Prince Donald Owuzi opened the debate. It centered on the new set of orders at the caucus meeting of the *Rapid-Life Association,* contemplating registration as a political party before the broadcast.

"But I think he made a point this time around, Sir!" The protem secretary of the association, Dr. Dan Duru added quickly "in the sense that he allowed for choices to justify ideological positions. Those of you who are just chairmen and governors without ideological commitments can now look truly political when you join any of the parties."

"What point? The government forming parties is a point? To ban the wisdom of the old, when politics is for matured minds with tested temperaments is a point? What point? The entire project will collapse, I can assure you. People form parties to form government. Government cannot form parties to form itself. This experiment will fail."

"You sounded like a prophet of doom again. Our problem is that we very often conceive of failure of a project before the implementation. The order may not be a package of perfect orders, but I think we should still go ahead and study them carefully before we react strangely. The ban on retired servicemen for instance, I think, should be welcome by all politicians. The generals, group captains and admirals are suffocating us and we should critically view their continued presence in our associations.

"These are men whose careers were enhanced from the national treasury. They fought no wars, quelled no riots and were never battle-tested, yet they rose to be administrators, governors, ministers, generals, marshals and commanders in the military. When they lost grip of power in the military, they turned to politics and disparaged our strategies just to get back to power. Since they can no longer organise coups or bear arms, they now use the politicians for an onslaught of another kind. How fair and logical does it sound? They storm our meetings with their full complement of military drivers and armed orderlies. Worse, the press goes after them for remarks and comments. I think that we are just being foolish if we fail to realise that our eventual success need not mean the continuation of the military in power by other means. We are fools," Dr. Duru was showing visible displeasure.

"But we all own this nation," Prince Owuzi maintained his stand. "Those of us 'selected' or 'voted' and the others yet 'unselected' or 'voted' need each other."

"Yes, we all belong here. But you can belong more than others. They were generals in the military, retiring to millions. Their junior officers, now in government, made them chairmen of viable banks and members of governing councils of viable parastatals, making it possible for them to continually keep the economy in their vaults.

"They stray again to hijack politics from us and pretend to belong to the anti-military establishments. And these are governments they helped to install and from where they are constantly consulted on security, budgetary and contract details. I think that Baguludu did this one well. *Haba!*"

"But, Dr. Duru, remember we most often invite them to be used as cannon fodders. How many of us politicians can be resolute and blunt in our utterances and statements as they often are. At rallies, we parade them to obtain permits. At our meetings, their aides are there to identify the security penetrating our fold. During visits to governors or the head of state, their mere presence give the required immediate security clearance for limitless access to such high corridors of power. You may be making a point. Yes, I think you are, but it is our fault, not theirs. We are a jittery lot. We want democracy without a drop of sweat or blood. With the new realisation, the military has always been in government since independence. You have adequately captured the horrible hold of the military on all areas of our national life. It is a tragedy, and the disguised horror is that we all sat back, completely ignoring the stench and choking smoke their presence has brought to everyone," Prince Owuzi looked drenched in the new realisation that made for some steam-letting.

But the age limit for the president was another case for national outrage. Many aspiring young talents became sidelined by the new order and reputable old hands equally fell by the wayside with the intricate details of the orders clamping bans for various offences listed, or the mere holding of positions in past republics. The consensus was that the orders were meant to restrict all retired military officers in their race to completely take over the government-formed parties as flag bearers.

The dialectics of an emerging democracy was manifesting negatively right from the stage of conception. Besides, another wrong foot was put on the race-tracks again with the order that the nation's *First Man* must not be less than fifty. There happened to be no account in history from which a parallel could be drawn. As best as it appeared, it was another punitive pendulous swing against a political class without uniformity in conduct and approach; an oddity in a national political life that must be disturbing Socrates in his grave.

The immediate past president of the largest democracy on earth after which our nation patterned all endeavours, was far less than fifty when he assumed office. William Pitt, son of the Earl of Catham was prime minister of an imperial power at less than twenty-five. Armed uprising overthrew General Batista in Cuba to pave way for Fidel Castro to be prime minister at the age of thirty-two. Emperor Nero became head of the Roman Empire at thirty while Jesus Christ, the symbol of Christianity, started his ministry at thirty. In fact, a military head of state before Baguludu became the nation's number one at thirty-three. Dr. Duru was not at home with that segment of the latest orders.

"I wish to restate again that, to make it work for the good of all, it does not have to be executed by a sage or a know-all general. The Kulaka of the former USSR, the noblemen of France and the Lords of Britain made their countries great in all spheres without much ado about the arithmetic of age. They never saw those they lorded it over as disgruntled, anti-democrats, insurrectors or enemies of progress whose excesses can only be curtailed by a sage."

"You see it that way Doc.?"

"Oh yes. But if you want these boys to go, obey their orders like zombies," Dr. Duru advised.

"But we can protest. We can use the human rights groups and the pro-democracy associations. They will bring down this government in just a few days. See what petrol scarcity did to them. They were jittery. The problem is that we very often fail to sustain the tempo of our protests. That's all," Prince Owuzi came bubbling again in agitation.

Dr. Duru was puffing off on his pipe where his attention had just shifted. He surveyed the room to ascertain a quorum for the meeting before turning to the prince for another lecture.

"Prince, if someone attempts to goad you into a demonstration, don't just try. Opt out quickly. You read today's papers that a new Inspector General has been appointed? Mr. Isaac Lagba is now the IG. Baguludu removed Okoh Fatunlah because the man opposed his broadcast at the council meeting. So they say. But I know it contained some elements of truth. Isaac Lagba is a riot man. He commanded the *MOPOL* unit for four years as *DIG*. He will play a good boy to Baguludu and will use everything to do any job to please him. And when we create panic and chaos, the army boys will merely advance the excuse that the transition was derailed by politicians and that the timetable needed a re-arrangement. Forget all the pro-everything around town and pray that all politicians plan and pursue, honestly, their strategies to take over power..."

He was cut short by a sudden push at the door that revealed four armed policemen bursting into the room with all force. In a flash, they had taken strategic positions with guns ready on cock. All together, fifteen men were gathered for the caucus meeting of the *RLA* to discuss the new developments following the broadcast. The Superintendent of Police that led the team to the secret venue accosted Prince Owuzi and was very dry with his questions.

"You know that this gathering is illegal, Sir?"

"No! We are just having a friendly meeting here."

"And you know that all associations have been banned or you didn't listen to the broadcast?"

"I did, but no guidelines yet for registration as party members. We must also see where our thinkings tally with the created parties and we are just..."

"Shut-up! Go to the Electoral Authority. This meeting is illegal. This assembly is unlawful! I have orders to dislodge everyone. Before I count three, everyone must disperse or you have yourselves to blame! One............, two............"

The room was empty in a flash. You do not joke with the orders of a man with a gun.

The realignment of ideologies to meet the manifestos of the government-created parties was come-easy-go-easy. Like-minds teamed up en-masse to either move left or right. Those with fervent dislike for the two extremes stayed at the middle of the road. There was enough ideological confinement for everyone. Police harassment was just a strategy to politically dislodge some people the regime had vowed to disqualify at all cost. The Baguludu regime kept a close watch on the parties and their members with a view to effecting surgery if and when necessary.

The party conventions were open courts for the trial of national morals and discipline. Probity and discipline fell flat as all positions, including party chairmanship were given to the highest bidders. It was an auction. Complex administrative details and directives took the time of the Electoral Authority that would have played the sniper to gun down the wrong beneficiaries of the auctions before they moved out with their wares. Another national mistake was rolled over like a project lacking in adequate supervision. Like an architect, General Baguludu knows the houses he was building and the tenants to put in them. Unwanted tenants may lose deposit and power of occupancy. He did it for the governorship race and the plans are carefully being extended to party elections.

*   *   *

The local hot lines of the head of state and military president are not known to many. Only very close friends come through them; and the subjects must be very urgent. That morning, the chief press secretary was on his normal early morning briefings with General Baguludu when a call came through.

"Your Excellency!"

"Yes, who is this?"

"Ah! General, even in a babel you can't pick my voice?"

"Oh! Chief, how are you today?" General Baguludu recognised the voice of his close friend, Chief Awari Aleti, the businessman-politician who recently indicated his intention to run as flag bearer for the Leftist Party amidst protests by party members who saw him as a rightist.

"Morning, General, and how is your family?"

"Fine, Chief, I was just receiving my morning press briefing about developments in politics nationwide, and your item is number three on the list. Surprising! You didn't even discuss this with me before you let it out."

"My General, you know the proverb of our people which says that the bridegroom before whom the bride is still coming to prostrate and lie flat for action must not attempt to trace the entry course of that bride by peering over the fence! You are the ultimate. You own me and I own you. We are one, and over the years, we have complemented each other's ambition and aspirations by all means. This project is your project. As *Olorioko* is concerned, you even have the final say and I know that I am save with you! *Abi I lie?*"

"Well, Chief, are you contesting?" there was dead silence and the distance between the two seemed beyond the normal one thousand and ten kilometres separating Amuta and Lapas. What was actually his reason for taking leave of his vast business empire with considerable investment in all areas of life and all over the world to mount the soapbox and race to the *Rocky*

Villa in Amuta? Was it the realization that political power was the ultimate with the unparalleled propensity to reverse even the most tremendous economic power? Was it just on the excuse that many representations to him about his ability to lead must not be rebuffed? Maybe it also had to do with his knowledge of the machinery of government. If these boys could effectively hold on to the aparatchik of state, then why not him? He was liked, loved and endowed! The thoughts came in series.

"General, I love to serve! I love to serve this country in another capacity and now is the time. You remember that old adage which says that vows are made only when their times are right and ripe. This is the time, General, for me to serve," Chief Aleti explained.

"Chief, I think you must not contest!"

"Why, General? I am not in any of the categories banned! Why?" He was bewildered.

"You are not banned, you are above fifty and can finance your campaigns from party convention and primaries to the national polls comfortably, but I still think you must not contest. Remember you are a creditor of government, Chief? Besides, this is not our agreement on my intentions."

"Yes, but I am not forcing you to pay now to enable me finance my electioneering expenses. No, I won't do that. General, you must give me your support. You are sounding very distant on this issue!" Chief Aleti muttered as some lines of sweat rolled down his temple. He took off his cap to be able to absorb the shock from General Baguludu, his closest friend for many years.

"First, Chief." Baguludu opened up again. "Why did you suddenly become a leftist? I used to know you as a rightist. I was briefed about happenings at the convention."

"My people said I must pitch camp with the winning team, and I am assured of success. But this development, I must confess, is worrisome. When you are out and I am there, there is no difference and no cause to worry!"

"No, I am only advising. Your people want you, not because you genuinely wish it. That's the difference between us. All the votes from your people cannot ensure national victory. Those you call your people are just twenty-four percent of the population, although they are the largest of the thirteen major ethnic groups making up our total count of over one hundred million. I don't see how you can rely on that and win. It has never happened before. Besides, I am scheduled to dissolve cabinet and the Revolutionary State Council (RSC) next week. I will still be president or head of state, but a transitional government will be sworn-in to be headed by a chairman. Our choice of chairman is from your local government. In fact, your ward. Let your people know that government is not a family business. He cannot hand over to you. Do you understand?"

"My God! But you didn't tell me this before, General?"

"I am not bound to tell you government decisions since you are not part of government. This is done to save you of the funds, time and energy to be expended."

"But if I go ahead and the people give me their mandate...?"

"Try and see, but I have warned you!"

"General......General.....General," the line went dead.

152

"This is strange. General dropped on me. This is strange."

And it was strange indeed. It never happened in their twenty years of association that had yielded vast economic advantages to both. Rumours were even rife that their eldest children were to be joined in wedlock, to cement the family closeness, with a deep knowledge of their high and low points. What got into General Baguludu? Not because he knew through the papers. Definitely not. Security reports must have made enough briefs available to the *C-in-C* too early. Not because his friend thought he made much from government to turn round and use same to seize power. After all, the General and his cohorts who seized control of government and goaded people to submission equally used the resources of government to achieve their aim. The head of state must be afraid of something, most probably his stolen billions. What could have been the concern of the chief with the leadership or chairmanship of a transitional council that will not be elected but merely appointed?

The mere mention of the general's reservations to the contest was bad enough, but not too bad to discourage him and thereby withdraw his candidature which was taken at peak auction, a normalcy in national politics, at the just concluded party convention. Chief Aleti had constantly thought that his country needed a man not persuaded to reluctantly accept the mantle of leadership, only to get there to loot the treasury, just because he saw the opportunity to enhance the status of his family and friends forever. He simply saw himself as the best of the lot in the race, and as such, was determined to break the jinx that no person from a particular part of the country could come to power via the ballot box or through a direct military coup. The General's reaction was a shriek, designed to cow and herd him back to hibernation. But do we have to lock ourselves indoors because of the shrills from the spirit of death prowling the streets? When we eventually overcome the fear, death must have dispatched all able-bodied men and women to the great beyond.

The prodigy of our life is already glaringly imminent in all areas of national life. Corruption has eaten deep into our social fabric that even children now ask for 'egunje' before obliging to run errands. The security agencies openly pick bribes, and display them in cellophane bags. Health institutions are just structures without facilities and institutions of higher learning are no longer baking any worthwhile graduates. Everyone is now a local government. You struggle to secure a land at great labour. You build the road to the site, erect your house, lay your water pipes after a borehole, buy poles and cables to be connected with electricity and thereafter, rates and bills of various shades and forms are rushed in for settlement. This is definitely not a way to make people happy and it is hardly a way also to give a sense of patriotism and exhibit a commitment to work more relentlessly for national growth. He must not yield to blackmail. The contest must move ahead. It is too late to withdraw. Too late.

"The President surprised me," the Chief told the Leftist Party caucus a few days later. "If..."

"Ah! But we need the support of the President!" the party chairman, Barrister Lam Zohor added quickly.

"Definitely, we need his support, Sir. These military boys can spring surprises anytime. They can disqualify, extend transition, change programme content, and withhold results for manipulation or for outright cancellation. They are a very dry set of human beings without emotions; a profligate, educated more in the ways of women, wine, gambling and looting. They are so insensitive to the time, the energy and the volume of money expended on anything. See what they are doing with the payment for contracts. The banks run after you but the khaki boys just push you around while they pay their retired generals," the party secretary, Dr. Duru, summed up the inhuman propensities of the military.

"We must seek audience with the President and obtain his formal approval for the success of a friend. Our strategy may sound excellent, but the execution may be faulted to an extent that we will be painted as incompetent."

"But, is that necessary?" Chief Awari Aleti chipped in. "Baguludu is my friend and I know that he hates speculations and the idea of being seen as favourably disposed to a friend. I think that we must go ahead with all party rallies and primaries. If we win convincingly, Baguludu cannot say we did not win! All we have to ensure is that our margin of victory is wide enough that we will not need him for any favour and we must work hard for the international observers to be reasonably convinced about our victory. I believe in my God who can do all things. An adage of my people says that 'if you have decided to go blind, make it pitch

dark, for partial blindness often results in rancour.' "
The Chief has a special appetite for proverbs.

"All the same, I think that we still need Mr. President.
You do not get to play with the feelings of a tenant
who is going to vacate an apartment for you. Besides, I
perceive a poisonous odour in the air! Do not make the
mistake that your friend will be honest with the result
of this election. Baguludu can say you did not win.
This may not mean anything to you, as you are too
rich to be poor again. But what about our party? We
need our party to make some other people rich," Dr
Duru tried to educate the chief and caucus members.

"That argument about the chairman of a transitional
council," he opened up again on a fresh breath of ideas,
"is too disturbing to me. We must know that the
government created this party and we have no basis to
quarrel with the *modus operandi* for a successful hand-
over. We can further deliberate on correcting apparent
mistakes from our own end. I am talking of mistakes
that arose as a result of developments from government
actions by the nature of the present dispensation. I
sincerely think that we can reconsider our choice of
flag-bearer in view of latest developments. To me, it is
illogical to produce a transition government chairman
and successively swear-in a new president from the
same tribe, state, constituency and ward. We have time
on our hands and we must re-plan within..."

"Dr. Duru! This is anti-party. Stop the blasphemy!"
Mr. Dan Bass, the party publicity secretary became
enraged.

"Take it easy!"

"No! Dr. Duru. You are getting scammy. And that is a wrong public relations approach to the success we envisage at the polls. In image building, consistency, personality illuminating statements and excellently running press liaison are very essential. We have laid all foundations and tested them successfully at the convention and the strategies made you to retain your position as party secretary when the *Rapid Life Association* died. We cannot go back on our choice without risking a slide in press and public assessment of our intentions, perceptions and seriousness in the conduct of the government business that we intend to control. We must not try this at all," Mr. Dan Bass was prepared to educate every member on the jeopardy of a sudden change in the party's presidential candidate.

"Do you agree that the risk is larger than the way you intend to...".?

"Doctor, I think you must stop dragging this. No one is here to discuss risks that you did not put in your agenda," the publicity secretary insisted.

"Why? The chief himself is here and the party chairman is on seat. Our success is what matters to the secretariat which I head, and not the level of placated agreements during meetings. I want the party chairman to remember the exact words of Lieutenant-General Koni Piyam, the chief of army staff, that the military is not sure of a successor out of the present crop of baby boom, and the un-repentant moneybags, grouping and parading as politicians. And he quickly added that the gaze of the military is on some people. Then, where do we fall? We must ask ourselves this question against the backdrop of the telephone conversation with General Baguludu by our flag-bearer. We must think and refuse to be sentimental," Dr. Duru was actually thinking in line with the party chairman.

"I see! I see," the party chairman, Barrister Lam Zohor nodded severally to the submissions which he saw as reasonable and well articulated. He did not mince words either, as he expressed his scepticism on the little excuses that could be blown wide open by the military.

"These are serious issues that no member must doze over. We are in politics to win and to control the machinery of government. It is not to truncate acceptability by the people without victory and thereafter retire to our homes, waiting for another opportunity. Honestly, I fear these boys who care less about how things are done outside the '*Part One Orders*'. Chief, why did you call him in the first instance?" Barrister Zohor demanded.

"We......we........we......well..." it was a clear case of stammer! "He is my friend and we talk regularly. A call at this..."

"Chief," the party chairman cuts in again, "you should have allowed a delegation of the party to visit the General on the occasion of the collection of nomination form and we would have used the occasion to formally introduce you publicly.

"The arithmetic of politics is basically that success is most often based on group advantage. You must realise that you are now a political foe to your best friend and business associate. He willingly told the nation about a terminal date but who is sure about his seriousness of that terminality? It was incredible to him that his best friend would declare interest in his post. As for the flag bearers of the other parties, maybe he could see their case differently, but for you, this is the reality on ground now. We need a more tactical approach which you have bungled, Chief. Starting this way is not too good for us, in spite of the people's goodwill and support in our favour. But like the publicity secretary has noted, we are already in public glare and we must do everything to stay ahead in the media blitz to be able to win convincingly." Great jitters showed in the chairman, but he had to rely on the proper use of the media to advantage and to obscure all flaws, including top-level disdain for the party's flag bearer.

"Thank you, my chairman," Chief Awari Aleti finally came up with words. "I accept whatever blame that is apportioned and if you want me to step down, I will gladly do that without grudge. You must know that I do not make my social outings contingent on the garment still in the loom. If you want me to play along, I am still available since we already have the support that will take us to a convincing victory. However, in view of the development on hand, I must say that we need to use all our hearts, brains, muscles, spirits, spleen and vision to further project the Leftist Party as the people's party. The unanimous trend with which we have been accepted by the electorate leaves me to wonder daily if ours will not be the ruling party for decades to come."

"Yeees! Yeeees! Yeeeees!!!" members chorused, briefly interjecting the LP's presidential candidate before he continued.

"I must again stress that our advert timing, copy focus and direction matter considerably. We have to focus on party programmes alright, but our candidate needs the rightful accolades to dwarf the two other candidates. Volunteer adverts are already running in the press but as we appreciate every gesture of goodwill, we must properly align our advert strategies.

"We must meet the press constantly, since press conspiracy is the charm of social and political success. Our advert must have rhythm. They must be well dressed, well spoken, well laid and organised to show a degree of clerical gaiety needed for party carriage and style. I am not a pressman, but I recognise a good story and advert when I see one." The silence in the room was captivating. One advantage of this candidate is that he talks infectiously. People listen to him when he talks and on this occasion, a loud sigh and comment from one of the members sent the entire members into a long fit of laughter.

"My President-in-waiting, Sir. You can talk my wife into adultery."

"Chief does not need that. Some other things can do the talking," the publicity secretary cuts in.

"What thing?" the member who had just spoken demanded.

"Money of course! And it is already talking in politics. Remember the way some people auctioned their conscience at the party convention? Government *option* failed and our own *auction* triumphed. Allah, I think we have the best of the best candidates. Baguludu can go and die," the publicity secretary insisted.

If Baguludu had to die, he had enough armour at the *Rocky Villa* to make it happen. Definitely not on the orders of a charge and bail publicity secretary of a government created party, who refused to see that his own candidate was equally a product of an illicit auction. The members of the LP caucus were mere singers of a loud chorus, but the silent notes underground are known only by a few.

order apocalypse

"... all that he touched became a harvest but the storehouse was
shut"

Politics is the most prolific breeder of all human endeavours. In attempts to gain and retain power and credibility, politicians stumbled into enduring mistakes and the same old tape was unwinding for the Leftist Party.

Dr. Dan Duru was not too amused at the unwinding scenario. To him, people were just living in glass houses and throwing stones at all directions. However, details of the national campaign tour were more important than the digressions pursued in euphoria of thoughtless speed. He had carefully divided the country into eight zones. To the party secretary, if you deal with the military, your strategy must be put in proper shape since military boys regard life situations as war endeavours which allow for the uprooting of populations, destruction of ambitions, deposition of kings or leaders and the consolidation of territories. Such dreadful deeds must be properly addressed to forestall a parallel in a transition agenda by a regime rumoured widely as not too keen in relinquishing power. The glamour of the military was to have a firm grip on its conquered territory, however violently the people protested.

Dr. Duru's strategy for the LP was to sufficiently whip up frenzied sentiments on democracy at rallies, thereby putting the khaki boys in an uncomfortable corner to guard against reneging on their promises. His strategy paid off during the long campaign tour that took the party to all nooks and crannies of the country.

"If his *'Insha Allahu'* is *'Insha Allahu'*, then we are close to living in the comity of civilized nations." Chief Aleti told the crowd at one of such rallies in the eastern town of Ebanu, the headquarters of Zone Four for the LP campaign train.

"That they have democratized in the local governments and the states is not the joy. The glamour is to enthrone democracy at the centre to enable us attend and be part of many international assemblies, and consequently end these years of isolation. They asked not to be rushed, we didn't rush them. They banned many politicians, we did not complain. They proliferated structures that wasted our fund, we just kept our peace and watched, unshaken in our hope that we will regenerate lost funds and fortunes."

The dais was large enough and was able to contain the idiosyncrasies of the entourage that raged with shouts, clenched fists and deafening feet-tapping to *ad-hoc* dance sessions in flowing cascading robes. Chief Aleti was at his best, working the crowd to frenzy.

"What did they not do? Our national currency is now a toilet paper; a worthless legal tender. The governor of this state, who is now one of the very great pillars of our party, even though he was elected on zero party basis, has wept three times in public as a result of the excesses of the military. Weep on, governor; one day the tears will stop!

"What did they not do? They prevented us from taking part in the last World Soccer Events, even when they know that national grief is usually put into limbo during sports meetings. What did they not do? We are now a country of hoodlums, made so by the inclement economic weather. Our oil sells, our treasury is full, but those who came to deceive us as redeemers loot them daily. The best cars, best houses and private jets are owned by these special classes of *civil servants*. What did they not do? Oh yes. One great thing they did not do is that they could not run the business of government progressively. The Leftist Party is here to do it. We will honour all international obligations, but we can no longer commit our men to keep peace at the risk of death and resource wastage in other countries while we wallow in squalor, want and disease. We must win. We have set out to win and no stopping." He concluded and the ovation rocked the dais.

It was a powerful speech, but the type Dr. Duru, the party secretary constantly warned him against. The secretary did not like the latest speech, insisting that Chief Aleti was playing the cow, constantly parading the slab when the butchers were set for the kill. He told the chief that to run a nation was not like running a business empire, where you fire one worker today and another is applying to be considered for same job tomorrow. As the entourage moved to the hotel, Dr. Duru made his discontent clear.

"Chief, you are not minding your language and you know that the security agencies are there to report their findings."

"Yes, but we were addressing a political rally and we must tell them what they want to hear. They, not Baguludu and his boys will vote for us to win, I must tell you that I am not afraid of death. Although life is so beautiful that it makes death appear horrible, but everyone must die one day." The chief was blunt.

"The people will vote, but the Baguludu boys will process the inputs. Watch what you say, Chief, and know where to stop."

"Then do we just give them money and forget the jaw-jaw?" the Chief was as tough as ever. "Let me touch everything and everyone and see what the harvest will look like."

"Chief, all that I am saying is that if you call the army names, the army will call you and the party names. And since they own the entire government machinery for now, you will be at a disadvantage and this will affect us considerably. The way I see it is that you are holding on to the bayonet and the nozzle of a gun, leaving the butt and the trigger to the army while at the same time calling on the referee to flag off a fight. That way you zero-out your own chances for victory from the onset as well as those of your supporters. If your touch produced a large harvest and the store house is shut against you, what happens?" Dr. Duru was clear in his ideas, but the Chief was uncomfortable with his modesty. He must sound and appear to be in control of the entire party machinery and capable of being held responsible for his actions. The central issue in the campaign must be the army, the beginning and the perceived end of national degradation.

"Baguludu is a farce. He cannot do anything to this election. The international observers are already here. The entire world is aware. Mobilization is at its peak. This government has spent much money, and the people know their president already. Tell me, why do you fear just one man in a pool of one hundred million men? They have cleared me for this election and I have no fear of failure or disqualification. If they mess up, we will mess them up too. After all, we know how they got there."

"Yes, Sir," Dr. Duru stopped arguing.

*   *   *

The President became inaccessible to all flag-bearers since the beginning of the race. Attempts to reach him were always thwarted by his aides who advanced various excuses. It was on deliberate instructions, but he was abreast of all developments in national politics through his transitional council members. He had told them at inauguration that their six-month stay was to ensure a free and fair election without the involvement of military high brows in the electioneering process. The chairman of the council, who was picked from retirement, actually came from the same ward with the Leftist Party candidate. In the actual sense of the matter, the Transitional Council Chairman, Chief Joel Shogbade, played prime minister while General Baguludu was president. By understanding, under this arrangement, a faltered or faulted election supervised by the unlabelled prime minister may be trashed into the dustbin of history along side the entire council, allowing President Baguludu to call for a fresh election. The trap was bare and the game was sure to stray into its bare fangs to enable Baguludu to continue in office.

Why did the president choose to pick a chairman from the same ward as the Leftist Party candidate? If the party came up with its choice first, why did government not appoint a similarly competent person from the remaining competent and willing others? Policy mishaps or rather, *dribbleries* were the greatest hallmarks of the Baguludu regime and a study of the regime is a study of hourly absurdities as constantly claimed by the people. The idea was to castrate the leadership of the Leftist Party by other means not connected with giving orders. He had carefully avoided such orders at the past meetings of the new council.

The transitional council was meeting for the seventh time since it came into place under the new dispensation. The security report on the coming national assembly and presidential elections, were the high points for discussion with the president and the report was too focused on the leadership of the Leftist Party and the future of the country. No negative reports were raised on national assembly aspirants. The zoom was on Chief Aleti.

The report was hard on the party's campaign strategy and the toxic content of the campaign rhetoric of Chief Aleti. It was a startling revelation of the very close details of his campaign tour, on which the security agencies showed no sentiments. The security painted, as not too slim, the pitiable razor-thin chances of the presidential aspirant moving close to his grade of envisaged success, the landslide grade. But how desirable it was for Chief Aleti to be given the chance to walk the red carpet to the exalted chair to be left vacant was the decision of the transitional council, in consultation with the President. The details of the report were too uncanny, especially on the Leftist Party candidate. It portrayed him as an affluent bully that fanned the flame of hatred against the military in all venues of his campaign, alleging much administrative incapability and devilish machinations against a government from which he was expected to take over power.

He was said to be too unwieldy in his speeches and addresses. Separate security monitoring groups on his trail were unanimous that he was likely to bring about a new national conflict and calamity if not checked or, better still, stopped. Maybe the security high ranks schooled them before they were sent on his trail.

His strategy was said to be too dangerous for the over four hundred ethnic groups that had lived together in harmony since the beginning of the century. The political disagreements he was trying to generate may burn too deep without a cure pill in sight.

"My Director of Military Intelligence was modest in his report, Sir," the secretary of defence told the president.

"This report is again inconclusive in view of the fact that Chief Aleti is a good friend of Mr. President.

Honestly, the security has its own idea about the entire election, but the feelings and friendly sentiments of Mr. President are also competing for consideration in our conclusion," he submitted.

General Baguludu was not an inch moved. The head of transitional council sitting by his side engaged his focus. He nodded him to take over the talks and stand sentinel for the impending doom of his kinsman.

"I will rather abide by the decision of Mr. President on this matter, Sir," the head of the transitional council muttered.

"Why? Your people are already alleging that you are a mere figurehead. A number two without a tool."

"They are ignorant, Mr. President. Only Number One carries the wand, I am Number Two!"

"Well, let's hope that they cultivate some more tolerance. We will waste the history of our struggle and the colour of military intervention to build a good foundation for the country if we abandon politics to those that are bent on such a path of waste and destruction like Chief Aleti.

"Anyone wishing to build more on the foundation of democracy, being put in place, must not attempt to undermine such democracy by violent actions and utterances. The report before us is an illustration of the rot in our national soul as to what to do right immediately. We behave badly always because of this rot. The conclusion of this report must not be influenced by my association with any candidate," Baguludu summed up.

"Our conclusion, Sir," the secretary of defence cuts in again, "is that this election should be postponed. The parties will then be re-organized and new candidates chosen. That way, we can re-arrange our programme and still maintain our credibility."

"No! Mr. head of council, what do you think?" President Baguludu threw his resolve to Chief Shogbade again for a final joint decision. Again, Shogbade was evasive.

"I think you are right, Sir."

"Let the electoral authority go ahead with the arrangements. Chief Aleti will not win any election. What Chief is having is another *Boxing Day*, and people are ready to take any money from his boxes full of notes. They did that with him before when he was a die-hard rightist and a major financier of the then ruling rightist party that we overthrew. We will not stop him. He will stop himself but just keep him under close monitor by drenching him in a phalanx of security. Like a violent fire, he will soon burn himself out and dance himself lame."

"And if he won, Sir?" the secretary of defence asked General Baguludu.

"I do not think he will win. He is accusing us of '*plunderphobia*' with brilliant noise all over the place. We will make our own very useful noise very soon by exposing his own '*contractmania*'. The government has a way of going about its business of human conversion. We may tamper with the entire process and this is a joker we must securely hide!"

Sitting arrangement at the council chamber was in alphabetical order of the various ministries. The ring-out was from table one, Chief Emasoga of the foreign ministry.

"Your Excellency, I think that we must stop the election from taking place. That way, our embarrassment will be manageable. We won't be able to manage the crisis of a sudden cancellation if the election took place. The best approach is not to allow any voting. That way, we will stem sympathy outbursts and the propensity for anyone to cause trouble."

"The election must hold!" the president insisted as it was always the case with him. "The electoral authority must go ahead. That is my position."

These types of orders make nightmares. Orders that would consequently recall national errors of the past, hunt the present and even drowse the future in unquenchable inferno of ethnic hatred. A kind of endemic war that is never ending, with all actions of government to strike a bargain capable of being construed as adding poison to an already bad situation. The belligerent director of army intelligence whispered additional information to the president and his countenance changed immediately. He lifted his body, drew his number one to position and announced sternly:

"Anyone who decides to make himself a martyr by fighting this election as a Jihad can go ahead. But I want to warn that the army will not stop at mere tear gas and rifle fire to keep law and order. We will fire mortar rounds, if necessary. Anyone who wished to stand erect must not forget his legs, and I must say that no aspirant can be bigger than the country. I will not stop the election. We are already committed, but I reserve the right to evoke the provisions of section four, sub-section seven of the electoral decree that vested the final decision in me, in the event of any development considered undesirable by government. The conception, birth, child-hood and adulthood of the next administration is a task that we must accomplish the way we want it."

"Your Excellency," Chief Emasoga continued with his pestering. "The international community is what bothers me. Our estimation counts in the event of a convincing victory that may be uneasy to ignore and which you may decide to ignore. Chief Aleti is powerfully connected and the foreign ministry may find it difficult to explain to the international community, Sir."

"You are not in charge. That's the job of Dr. Zuma of the information ministry and he was re-appointed as Secretary of Information. I do not see any reason for all these. Chief Aleti will not win! Even if the 'outernational' community is watching, we are the one who can best describe what is good for us," General Baguludu was resolute in his decision.

Dr. Zuma was too distant during the debate by the transitional council members. Too busy within the past few weeks as he had to face the press constantly to justify new government actions. He had to rationalise the schedule of the electoral authority as plans unfolded too rapidly and constantly. He held parleys with directors of organisation of the parties on the purity of campaign promises as they relate to the reality on ground. He was actually very close to the ground and could thus speak from a position of strength.

"Your Excellency," he opened up. "Within the past few weeks, I have been able to discover that the campaign train of Chief Aleti, the Leftist Party candidate, often became infectious anywhere it went. Politics is still largely an auctioneer's game and the Chief runs auctions, since he has all the wherewithal. The future is nothing to our people. Only the money on hand is something. The financial influence of Chief Aleti on the people is so much that I stand convinced that if the elections were held today, he is sure to emerge victorious. His nature and nurture have affected the national politics and his money is making everyone mad. The chief has something to sell and our people are buying it crazily. He is simply infectious. Admirers place free full page adverts, with a view to rubbing themselves into him and catch on the opportunity of his coming administration." Dr. Zuma took from the glass of water on his table and adjusted his microphone to gain more comfort.

"Conclusively, your excellency, my discovery as made known earlier, is that electioneering from party registration, campaign rallies, voting, to the change of guards, if it took place at all, will be the most potent bond with violence in this country. It could be a fiercely dividing factor that would daily aggravate group hatred, ethnic aggression and the cannibalism of our national image because of his use of obscene and vulgar political languages. Listening to Chief Awari Aleti in his rallies is just like swallowing acid. We are the worst for it, since the electoral authority will just clear anyone with millions, even if he never had any record of success in managing human resources, especially in government. I think that I will urge Mr. President to stop this election and allow more candidates to be re-screened for better choices," he suddenly rested his case.

"In fact, as rightly observed before now, the transitional council chairman cannot hand over to Chief Aleti, a man from his own constituency," the Secretary for labour, Alhaji Sule Jadah, put one over the submissions.

The issues at stake were gradually becoming multi-dimensional, all weighed against the perceived success of Chief Awari Aleti in the polls. The President nursed the grudge that as a very close family friend and business partner, he was not consulted before the Chief joined the race, even with the full awareness that President Baguludu was scheming to give up the khaki and continue in office. The consensus by the military top-notch also, was that he was a very worthy creditor of government by his daring exploit of Baguludu's connection in very high places. The political thinking equally disfavoured a situation whereby the president's choice of a transitional council chairman would hand over the reigns of power to a man from his own ward.

The conflict he constantly created between words and muscles gave the 'boys' the feeling that he planned to deal with the army constituency, a good reason for them to ensure that he must not win, at all cost. A large part of the findings against Chief Aleti was however never subjected to thorough high-level scrutiny by the security which was caught between its job and the closeness of Baguludu to the Chief with a pathetic conviction that General Baguludu may not easily sweep such closeness under the carpet. The moderate approaches adopted in their reports were capable of compounding the failures of both the president and his junta, as well as that of Chief Aleti in becoming the next civilian president.

Maybe the Leftist Party candidate needed to be understood. A political trickster alright, with limitless powers of persuasion, inducement and intimidation, he still needed to be understood. But for the security reports, maybe he was a victim of media-generated vices, which like bacteria, was multiplying and infesting everyone, including those to decide his fate at the polls. As things stand, General Baguludu was saying the security reports indicated that there was a real fear following a cry that was real. But was the cry real?

"Honestly I think I am sorry for my friend if the reports I receive daily are anything to go by. He has been deceived by a gang of dreamers acting as terrorist bombers who will pay no attention to whoever they take with them to the graves. I still stand by my decision not to disqualify him or to re-order a fresh election on excuses that I can tie up to security reasons. I will not do that. No!" General Baguludu was becoming very disdainful of the Leftist party flag-bearer at every moment.

"Government job, I insist, is different from private business. In one, the narrow interest of individual success and glory is paramount. In the other, the larger interest of groups with un-negotiable commitment to their well-being looms large. If these reports I have before me actually speak of the bottom line, then what

175

will the headlines look like when Chief Aleti gets to power? He can go ahead to say anything; after all, this is a period of campaign glut. That of action glut is on the way." And the second transitional council meeting rose!

"You cannot trust Baguludu. He may turn around and break the coconut on the head of anyone who worked against the success of his friend. One must learn to play safe", a security high-up noted to a council member on their way out of the meeting.

*   *   *

The Seers Ministry was not too known until television appearances made it a household name. Sixty minutes on national network every Saturday unfolded scores of miracles confessed to by those affected. Business, matrimony, parentage, afflictions, procreation, survivability and so many other aspects of life became areas with peculiar problems that got solved by setting foot on the Seers Temple in Lishi, the northern town largely inhabited by Muslims. Lishi became a pilgrimage centre with Christians all over the country, attempting constantly to meet the young evangelist, Bene Tiri, whose handshake sent you sprawling on the ground as the *Holy Ghost Power* would be instantly released into you.

A good complement of the human traffic was the monetary influx that came in the name of pledges, tithes, contributions, offerings, promises, helps etc. Chief Awari Aleti, the leftist party candidate, was rounding off his campaign rally in Lishi by honouring an invitation from the Seers Ministry to be special guest at the dedication of the new church auditorium, a fifty-million naira project begun just nine months before. It was a Saturday.

The Directorate for Military Intelligence met a day before to lay out strategies in conjunction with the Containment, Camouflage and Deception crew *(CCD)* for the monitoring, handling and prevention of chaos. Young Lt Col. Sanni Jibo who led the group was a directing staff in covert logistics at the Lishi Cantonment, from where the military take-over began. Then a Captain, Jibo was a core putchist. The dedication was envisaged to generate much fuss and the press would normally make a loud sarcastic yawn at the entire event if Chief Aleti again maintained his tirade on government. Censor must prevent him.

"But how do we edit an informal speech, Sir?" a junior officer wanted education as Lt. Col. Sanni Jibo gave final briefing at the venue.

"Simple! Just cut off the microphone and our man close to him will move ahead to stop him from talking. Alright?"

"Yes, Sir."

"Obey all orders and not just the last orders! Co-operate with him, but don't submit to him and don't create a scene for the press to sell their papers. We have warned the pastor against moves calculated to discredit the government. If he refuses to keep to it, he will have himself to blame."

And as mounted troops swarmed the venue, parading horsewhips and the best in police light armour, arrival was timely. Chief Aleti, with his entourage rode in his latest rover jeep to the dais and to the warm embrace of Pastor Tiri who ushered him to the microphone for his speech. He was toothy.

"This is the joy of stable polity. To move around freely in your country, engage in constructive dialogue with friends, and perform duties for God like what we are doing on this occasion, and have hopes for the future in fulfilment of life's aspirations and ambitions. But today, our hopes are gradually being pushed down the precipice!" Chief Aleti opened a new wave of political indictment of the military.

"We have been deceived for long and, even now that we are staking everything to bring back glory and dignity to living, booby traps are laid on all ways. If we escape them, it is because our Lord is good!"

"All the time..." the chorus sounded far into all corners of the environment with the church choir sounding a note in a cacophony of trumpets.

"This election, we will win. In fact, we have won. Our majority is certain in the National Assembly."

"Ameeen!" the follow-up became ecstatic again, and the choir gave the lead in "Winner o, o, o, winner.......!"

The next two minutes was a jerk-and-gig session of writhing, grinding and dancing. The drums boomed, the trumpets blared and the guitars roared like the ceaseless crash of sea waves on beach sand. The CCD team became lost temporarily in the religious euphoria.

"My God!" the LP candidate resumed after the sweep of the *Holy Spirit* unleashed by the chorus. "This is the glamour of democracy; the glamour of personal usefulness to the service of God and to one's nation. Militarism is nothing! Yes, nothing! It is a conspiracy of the unruly."

"Oh. yes!" the crowd roared again and Dr. Duru used the diversion to nudge his presidential candidate to moderation. It was ignored as usual.

"They are at it again. The devilish innovators are again scheming for their selfish ends. I appeal to you to seriously guard against anyone, however highly placed, attempting to invalidate your vote. That single vote is a giant step to an enduring democracy. Give it freely to the LP and fight resolutely to ensure that it is not consigned to wastage. We have wasted too much political energy and have been frequently goaded into dissipating personal energy on a group, without results. Having spent much time, energy and money, we are again being hinted by this group that the government may disqualify. Who they plan to disqualify I do not know, but the turmoil will be great. They are already jittery and we will visit their sins. Yes, we will, but by restitution and not by retributions. If the United Nations..." Chief Aleti's voice trailed off. He hissed, spat and bellowed mouthful hellos into the microphone a few times and gave up.

Dr. Duru was at hand again with his caution. He must have sighted Lt. Col. Jibo at a distance and rationalised the sudden failure in the address system to his covert directives.

"Chief, just announce your donation and move to your seat. What is the point shouting at an armed robber across the highway? You identify yourself and you risk being shot. You are giving away too much and if we lost this election, it will be because you never knew where and when to stop."

Lt. Col. Jibo ordered that life be restored to the wires with just a nod to his men and, suddenly, the speakers roared back to life and the "Praise Go-od!" was heard several metres away. Chief Aleti seized the microphone again and added more pep to the report of the *CCD* team scribbling away beside him and, in apparent disregard to Dr. Duru's advice, which he used as a campaign instrument immediately.

"My party secretary just whispered to me here that if an armed robber broke into your house, just be still until he has finished raping your wife, carted away your property and emptied your vault. Are we that docile?"

"Nooooo!"

"We won't wait for the United Nations to raise delegations and for human rights groups to issue relentless statements before we cast off this yoke. No military government is representative. They employ slave cabinet to deceive everyone and steal security votes. We must talk about them to be able to plan the future and the...". Dr. Duru again. He was too visible that you can almost pick his advice.

"Chief, talk about the opposition, not the military." And as usual, his advice was turned into a campaign material.

"Our people have a wise saying that if you come between a cobra and a mosquito, kill the mosquito first, even if you have to use a sledge hammer. Turn your back at the cobra and it will flee, but the mosquito will still race after you to suck your blood. Although truth is bitter, we must realise that the military is the mosquito and not the rightist party. It is a party without candidate. The rightist and the military are playing a game on you and me. The centralists are dead. We are the only party of the people and, with you; we are fighting the same battle to arrive at the same point of victory. It is that victory we are celebrating here with the dedication of this church to the glory of God and the usage of man for soul winning with a twenty million naira token. Thank you!"

The frenzy was infectious, and the ecstasy large enough to consume the frail. The church choir lifted every soul sky high with the Halleluyah chorus. Handel must have twitched at Westminster Abbey as his famous composition pounded souls and lifted them under vibrating skulls.

However, the greatest foes were really not the military, but street corner orators that extol all utterances, actions, steps and in fact, all moves by Chief Awari Aleti as divine. No one saw the actions of the LP candidate as politically awkward and lacking in all the finesse associated with his level of carriage in business and social status. Dr. Dan Duru was close to recognizing this. If politics were to be pure theatre, no one, and particularly the military that was to hand over, expected it to be a confusing baby-boom game that must become messy by every whisper, shout or a bark into the microphone at every street corner rally. The military had constantly claimed that it had no qualification to claim to be a political nerd, but it had the discipline to work out an order to regulate politics and very minimally challenged by its officers corps or rank and file. If it became messy, it was not because the orders were inadequate and inexplicit, but because compliance to orderliness was not part of civil life in our own peculiar setting which we very often compared with civilizations that got off the ground centuries earlier.

*   *   *

Only the head of the transitional council, the head of government and the electoral authority chairman punctuated the sea of gorgets at the Transitional State Council meeting dominated by service chiefs, general officers commanding and the military secretary.

The rightist party had rushed a petition to the *Rocky Villa*, alleging violation of the relevant sections of the electoral decree. They claimed that the Leftist Party candidate, Chief Awari Aleti, "mounted the soap box and addressed a rally at Lishi for two hours when the campaigns were officially scheduled to have ended an hour earlier, at midday."

The penalty was clear and precise, but to apply it was difficult. General Baguludu who came into council chambers with a swagger stick, for the first time, was toothy as usual and appeared decided on what course to take between justice and vengeance; two options that must necessarily carry the same level of public denunciation. They were, so to speak, better resorts than no actions at all. He raised his swagger with the brass end, pointing directly to the chairman of the electoral authority.

182

"You will not allow us to rest in our barracks. You have made us urban soldiers and our boys now complain of civil intrusion into their barracks and mess lives," the President passed his gaze from one civilian to the other.

"We thought your noise for change was informed by good reasoning and logic, but here you are. All campaigns must end at 12 noon, and a candidate still went ahead to hold a rally several hours later. What was the explanation, Mr. electoral chairman?" Baguludu was looking vindicated that his friend finally played into his hands.

"Sir, the Chief said that his party officially lodged an objection two months ago that rallies end at 12 midnight and not at 12 noon."

"Did you inform him that the decree would be amended to satisfy his wishes?"

"No, Your Excellency!"

"Then what are you recommending? The penalties are clear and why are you waiting?" General Baguludu asked sternly.

"Your Excellency, we have concluded elections nationwide. In fact, we are waiting for the last batch of results. We cannot disqualify now. Only the President can do that, and this is not even advisable since the candidate in question appears to be leading in majority of the states already collated."

"And then? Did you see this security report on him?" the President pushed a paper to him.

"Yes, Sir. The *LP* candidate registered in his home ward as number *MNR-00271*, but voted in Lapas at the booth nearest to his residence on a new card *SPR - 01347.* Clearly, a possession of two voting cards is an electoral offence, but the chief is your friend, Sir. You must decide everything, but remember we are too close to the finishing line to restart the race."

"My friend, you must stop further announcement of results. By the way, who told you the man is winning? Do you run an electoral process on press reports? A man raped your wife and you said you couldn't do anything because the woman was about to put to bed before you were told. These bloody civilians."

"You cannot draw that parallel, Sir. If the candidate..."

"Shut up! Who is drawing parallel lines here? Are we working mathematics? Go and apply the sanction alright. Stop the election immediately. Both presidential and national assembly elections must be stopped."

"I cannot do that, Sir. That is your exclusive preserve. The decree gave you that right, not me." The electoral authority chief insisted, playing safe to protect his name and honour.

"Then you must step aside for me to do it."

" Yes, Sir, but I have..."

"Shut up," the chief of army staff gloated from the right of the president and rolled up the sleeve of his number two as if looking for a convenient punch posture.

"These bloody civilians. *Haba!* You don't know that you must obey orders. *Sege! Barawo! Every time turenchi! Turenchi with C-in-C, Sege!*"

"*Bah Sege*, General. When you are too consistent in rolling out orders, you create an order-full society rather than an orderly society, thereby unintentionally creating a theory of chaos. This new order may be chaotic. We would have done it before now, and without labour, but Mr. President insisted that we go ahead with all electoral arrangements. To do it now is pure travail. I advise against it, even if I am going to step aside for the announcement to be made," the electoral chief was being evasive. He was ordered to bell the cat and not the dog.

They were truly bloody civilians, highly gifted in languid pace of development when a solution was urgently needed. Slogging through the difficult terrain of national consciousness with its attendant resentments and restlessness by the people, all military efforts would fade into years of wastage if last minute arrangements were not properly tidied up. But they needed the wastage to be shamed out of power.

After all, there is nothing in the law books expressly directing a military head to voluntarily give up power. Even if they exist, as the handiwork of the military, no military head must work or major in them, or be moved by the legalistic framework of international business, politics and social mores. The military is a pulsating profession with accruing tremendous economic advantages, resulting in the normal barracks and pepper soup syndrome fading rapidly for urban cruise in modern autos and ceremonial appearances in five star hotels. Baguludu cannot be indifferent.

But that is not to say that much of the military era was used for cutting ribbons, attending charity events, pinning rosettes and taking vacations abroad. It equally turned a land of groundnut pyramids and cocoa stores to waterways of crude oil armada.

If a stirring national destruction must be prevented, then the personality-propelled politics that had resulted in political dynasties must not be allowed to come near power again. Now was the time for the military to tinker with the election and General Baguludu took that pound of flesh from Chief Aleti. He showed him that government is powerful enough to give anyone anything he lacked as well as take away everything that he possessed.

*   *   *

The mast on top the onion dome at the national station in Lapas was beaming out the national bulletin at four in the afternoon when the green coloured army jeep approached the heavily fortified gate.

The young Lieutenant in army khaki looked like a scarecrow in the company of the heavily built driver and the press secretary to President Baguludu. They made their way into the cubicle from the director-general's office. Moving heartlessly in disappointment and despair, the Director General, Malam Bello Ukah, made the cut-throat signal for the announcer to stop the news delivery. After a rushed rehearsal, the interlude of music was stopped and the announcer came on with the message:

"Here is a special announcement from the Rocky Villa. The President, Head of State and Commander in Chief of the Armed Forces, General Ramos Baguludu, in consultation

with the Transitional State Council, has approved a cancellation of the on-going presidential elections.

All results declared so far are annulled and all those yet to be declared, voided. The electoral authority is hereby dissolved and the three parties disbanded. The Transitional Council has been directed to put in place the modality for another electoral body, with a view to organizing fresh elections in no distant future. Signed by the Press Secretary to the President."

The news item devastated the nation and Lapas. The sin of a city blew its core in four days of protests, riots, arson and destruction that left many dead and priceless properties destroyed. It was a state of absolute chaos and lawlessness at its peak. The military was taxed to the limits and the government chewed a mouthful of discomfort that it found too stony to swallow. International estimation and recognition sank, and sanctions replaced grants. It was a season of all odds against a government that became too unfortunate, dancing to a mixed tune in the adversities it helped to create by a cacophony of relentless orders.

The secretary for information, Dr. Amba Zuma, was most unfortunate in having to recreate and sustain an image for a leprous emperor. He told reporters at the end of a transitional council meeting that discussed the national chaos:

"No civilian president can become a General. Only a General can become a president or whatever he decides to become, or do whatever he wishes to do."

"Like annulling an election?" The *Post* reporter queried.

"Yes. And this spate of riot and violence will continue to undermine democracy and put progress in fetters."

"The government created the present state of chaos and instability. How do you plan to arrest it?"

"That, I don't know!"

And no one appeared to know what everyone knew. This satanic wedge in the national soul went ahead for weeks, and for the period it lasted, national vision was obscured and individual consciousness was blurred. What started for Baguludu in rallies and adulating statements suddenly nose-dived into chaos and repulsive group statements. His government was on ground but the entire gamut of administration he could no longer control and curtail. Daily events pointed to the fact that his ways were no longer pleasing unto the Lord and, consequently, his friends and foes were no longer at peace with him.

Leaders of the Market Women Associations nationwide converged in Amuta. It was not one of their usual uniformed outings to press home how the rural women must be treated with diverted funds meant for the improvement of infrastructures to serve everyone. This time, they came to confer and make plain, why General Baguludu must go.

The Great Conference Hall was filled up and as usual, wrappers and *ipeles* were spread across the green lawn to make for the normal funny way women take their seats without chairs. Hadjia Awawu Ligama spoke with the microphone very close to her lips as if to prevent any word from escaping unheard.

"Our President and General, Sir. These are mothers from all parts of this country. We have been with you since you came to power and we love you dearly. But events following the annulment of the elections have been too violent for us to withstand. We hold our two breasts daily as our sons and daughters got shot in the streets. *Haba*! People are dying and the most affected are the young ones. If they were soldiers, then the feeling would have been different. But they are not. We are just killing our future and God is watching".

"Hadjia? In any abnormal or war situation, people are meant to die. And this one, I didn't cause it." Baguludu sounded defiant.

"General, don't say that. Women are here and we are the mothers of the living. Although of one bone, we make the rest eight function. General, just take a look at the metal bowl by the platform. What do you see? Catfish. Seven mud water catfishes, brought all the way from Lapas to be presented to you by the Lapas Market Women Association. Ask your wife the significance. I used my status to stop them from doing any harm. Please listen to us General, listen to us. Try to prevent the curses of women losing their children and your wife losing you."

"How Hadjia?"

"By resigning! General, you must resign O! Allow the interim government appointed by you to organise another election. The chairman, Chief Joel Shogbade can do it. This country is burning."

"And you want Shogbade to step into the ruins of the inferno? Can he manage the situation?"

"Yes, General! When you step out, anyone can step-in. But the courage is in stepping out and stopping the present bloodshed. Don't play God. What you have is enough forever? Let God choose His candidate."

*   *   *

The emergency transitional council meeting went late into the night and the mood was by all standards too tense and charged. If Baguludu goes, who protects his vast political and economic interests? How does he empower a man he picked to be used for a transient purpose as a new Head of State? What happens to his plans and hidden agenda to transit from a military to a civilian president? The questions were long drawn and the answers were as confusing as the situation on ground.

"General, Sir," Dr. Zuma, the doctor of everything but the truth, broke the tensed silence. "To be able to have enough grip on the transitional council, I suggest that we agree to empower Chief Joel Shogbade and change the name to Interim National Government with General Sunday Abami as Vice-Chairman of the interim government, Sir."

"You too have agreed that I must go?"

"Eeeh, no Sir. But, you see, I mean that, after all..."

"Dr. Zuma, stop rambling. My wife has told me to go. Not anyone of you here, but I am coming back to operate from a position of greater strength. My commission is yet to be completed."

"Ah!" Dr. Zuma exclaimed.

The next day, Chief Joel Shogbade was sworn in and General Baguludu was silently moved out of the Rocky Villa without the traditional military pull-out ceremony. It was the case of a lion falling prey to the antics of a tortoise. The tempo of violence simmered down and all restlessness abated. At least, the situation has changed and Chief Shogbade must be allowed to prove his capability.

Little did anyone know, however, that his tenure was carefully worked out the moment he was sworn-in. He went in and got out as rapidly as he held meetings. Within three months, the interim government met fifteen times discussing nothing worthwhile. Chief Shogbade's vice-chairman was merely getting the files filled up to justify his ambition. At the sixteenth council meeting, he flooded the council chamber with battle-ready soldiers and forcefully obtained the document of resignation of the chairman of the interim administration in a bloodless coup.

It took courage to do it, and the new head of state assumed the euphemism of a brave hunter in the chaotic forest of one thousand crazy demons. Moreso for his propensity to steer a new course, by pulling down hitherto untouchable structures impeding national advancement as recognised only by the military. If the brave hunter knows what to do, how to do it and what the people feel about a new *Messiah* became the new set of worries.

The people were pacified principally because an undeclared life president was pushed out, and a selected interim leaders shoved aside with no life lost. The new man appeared to know the stage and the orchestra, but the concert plot and the stage was an issue for a new season in military-political adventurism, not known to the people. In actual fact, the orchestra was loud enough to be heard by way of his equally loud antecedents, but the chorus demonstrations deafened almost everyone. The popular thing was to stage rallies to welcome new leaders to power. Very often, people are however oblivious of the fact that from the beginning of creation, the popular things are never right and the right ones are never popular. All the same, the rallies soon became a daily event nationwide, in support of General Abami, a man everyone knew little about even when much was said about him.

motion for adjournment

"...bye-bye to the godless, goodnight to the godly."

The nation is not a strange bedfellow to military takeovers, cabinet changes, scramble for appointments, state house cringing and hobnobbing. Academics, politicians, businessmen and captains of industry play to the gallery on newspaper pages, television programmes and at phony rallies to have a bite at the cake whose baker no one cares to know. They jostle for positions as early as the khaki shirts with gorgets appear on screen.

The litany was not different again. Transition or not, the old government was gone. Annulment is nothing and no one ever lived by what was annulled. People lived by the essence, and in this instance once again, the clear essence was the new military government that came to power to stem the disaffection between the transitional council which was unceremoniously sent packing and the in-coming party whose victory was annulled in a conclusively 'inconclusive' election. To any stage-manager, a government was in place and human beings must run the affairs by applying for the positions. After all, military politics is by drafting, a fiat call to serve. Civil and military politics cohabited in the art of sharing, and if you are not there to share, people would take your own portion.

Of the over five hundred applications for ministerial appointments, the new helmsman, General Sunday Abami, seemed not too impressed by anyone. A queer soldier, he was not in a hurry to constitute a cabinet. Those interested in positions could pile up applications and curriculum vitae as they wished, but his choices were kept close to his chest and he approached each one personally to set sailing with him on the wreck-bound ship of state. Even those who, by their actions, urged him to commit regicide were not sure how deeper he was going to sink the ship of state. And he thoroughly wrecked the ship.

The long delay in announcing the cabinet sent tongues wagging. When finally the names came, it was telescopic of the full-length theatre for which the gallery was full. A great military leader that conquered both the man and his mind, General Sunday Abami possessed stone-cold discipline, excellent destructive ability through surrogates and an anvil-like control over his men-of-war. As secretary of the transitional council under General Baguludu, he manipulated the chaotic situation to oust his boss and the transitional chairman, seizing power to stifle all the apparatus of state economy, politics and administrative machinery. His attention to intelligence gathering was awesome.

It may be prophetic or not, but Bishop Joshua Lubaba again warned in a press statement, as the tempo of the usual rallies to welcome the General to power reached a frenzied height:

"The drum of adversity is sounding from a new hand. You can't stop dancing until the drummer takes a rest

which is far from being near, and the various dance steps and cacophony of voices will be of great historical importance long after his death. Watch this man."

For three years, the drumbeat was loud enough, the dance steps were various, the sonorous voices were relentless but the stage set-up was unchanging. The only change was perhaps that a toothy smile of inviting furrows was forced out of step, just as he was forced to annul the truth, and replaced by pitch-dark goggles through which General Abami winked negatively at everything human, honourable and worthwhile. Like his predecessor, he created phony parties for gullible and *'wakie'* politicians to join.

As against the military academy's code of conduct, this was an officer who performed top state functions, national broadcasts and the regular signing of death warrants, which he enjoyed, under dark goggles. A sower of poverty, want and death, General Abami established himself as a man with a full stomach but an empty mind. He ran a cabal that was primed to cope with short notices to kill, maim and destroy men and even children of those who made an improper heave at his devilish proposals.

It was a season of assassination of those who raised their voices too low or too loud. If by your actions, you were identified as belonging to the opposition, a funny idea in a military set-up, the bullet would whirl at your head. If your position is to *'sidon look'* at his excesses and directionless economic and political posturing, as made famous by an erudite politician, you risked being bombed. To escape a *Yunusa*, you must constantly be praising, giving adoration and wearing his tiny burst-badge by your left chest.

Charges about imaginary siege on the civil society and plots against the military were endless. The *bloody civilians* were constantly led to jail for raising their voices against the annulment of a free election and its replacement with a repressive rule. If you asked why a rightful ruler must be detained without trial, you were equally thrown into detention, moved from one prison to another and fed on twenty naira daily. In one of his budgets, reputed usually to come many months behind schedule, detainees' feeding suddenly disappeared from the police allocation. A bewildered Inspector-General asked him at the council meeting before the broadcast and he simply said no responsible government would spend public funds to feed activists and human rights campaigners in prison as this will amount to giving them more strength to continue to criticize.

"So, the IGP thinks that there must also be human right without a human left?" asked the General.

"No, Sir. I only think that detainees must be properly fed from the proceeds from their fatherland. After all, Sir, a detainee today may be a minister tomorrow." The IGP told General Abami.

"We are not here for that. If you want to be a human rights campaigner, put off your uniform and cut off your left arm," he sadistically urged the IGP.

Such was the nature of the thought of a leader of over a hundred million people. If you were lucky that the wind blew the sail early to expose his plan, you may escape into exile, and the number of exiles during

General Abami's few years reign of terror and horror far outnumbered that which history recorded for South Africa during her decades of apartheid rule.

General Abami tasted power and his immediate reaction, like his predecessor's was that only the sting of death could remove him. No one had attempted to trace his ulterior destiny in the hidden national history of the future. His intentions were to restore the parties, organise elections and win the elections for himself. What a mistake!

"After all, I did not annul any election," he told his colleague-in-sin at one of the guest houses at the *Rocky Villa* after the sessions, for which he had violent affection were over, and the exchange of pleasantries began over beer.

"You were in that meeting John. Did I talk when Baguludu was deciding? I just said *Segey Barawo* to the chairman of the electoral authority and that was all. "

"*C-in C Sir, that one don pas o. When dey court martial a dead soldier, na only him boot and cap go dey for table! Oga, make we drink and forget the past.*" Lt. General John Olisa tried to calm him down.

"Now, they are talking and talking. *Segey* again to everyone. They called me and said I was the only one who could safe the nation from the grip of Baguludu. The national dailies carried it as front page lead stories and everyone read it. They are just complaining for nothing. They told me 'come' and I came. Now they want me to go. Go where? Unless I want to go, nothing can remove me from power, *Allah*! Now, the chairmen of two of the political parties have told us

197

that they cannot win the election except they choose me as their candidate. People will have more to say." General Abami exhibited his new arrogance.

"Sir, the other parties have even said that their convention will also adopt you as a unanimous candidate. *Ah, dem go hallah.*"

"But John, what do we do with that man in detention? They are saying that the man won the election. I know, but the man is a security risk."

"*Oga, dat one nah sikurity matter. Abi nah you arrest am? Police say dey arrest one man wey broke law. Wetin concern you, Oga? You fit add IGP job for your own? When you don win election finish, who go remember another winner wey dey detention?*" the devil's disciple encouraged Abami.

"*Release that man, General, because we hear say the man get strong international connection,*" one of the ladies pleaded over a foaming glass of beer.

"*Shurrrr-up! No be only international, he get outernational connection self. Na politics you come talk for here or na money you come make? Just face your business,*" General Abami cowed her. But God was laughing at his presumptions just as He does daily with the presumptions of those who want to hold on to the power on earth or in a nation without first consulting the King above.

*　　　*　　　*

"What a man!" Bishop Joshua Lubaba told the 12th Annual Conference of Bishops held at Lapas.

"I warned the nation about this illiterate General. Today, this country is a shadow of itself. We declined under the dictator who opened new pages of history and wrote horrifying tales on them with human limbs and blood.

"The past three years under General Abami have been dark and bloody. If you have undeserved sudden power, there is the tendency to pretend and always behave under flashes of madness. For those who have run amuck once in their life to systematically seize power like General Abami did, they not only become deaf, they need flesh and blood not to degenerate further in their madness. Fortunately for him, he consumes flesh and blood daily. But his madness continues. He tries to show us every time that he is clever by tampering with everything and every situation.

"The traditional institution was tampered with by several depositions, pro-democracy groups were harassed constantly and their members killed or exiled. Educational institutions earmarked for some particular locations were suddenly taken to places where study was regarded as a hard labour. Several imaginary coups were 'uncovered' and culprits sent to jail, after narrowly escaping execution. Politicians have been asked to join any of the six political parties he created for himself or go back to their businesses. This is the first head of state that doubled as a crude oil merchant, a leader who delights in importing what we have abundantly while exporting what the nation lacked direly.

"How, for God's sake, can a man create six parties and be a flagbearer for the six? However, the bad administrative misdemeanours General Abami is teaching us might lead to the discovery of what a denial of our freedom could mean; *having faith in God*. Even when he ordered the creation of six political parties and made himself the presidential candidate of all of them, you must know that God is watching, and will not vacate His throne for him."

Bishop Lubaba was too blunt at the forum. Journalists usually covered the opening ceremony and quite a handful was around.

"I sympathise with the wives and children or your colleagues who have been incarcerated for these many years by the Abami regime. For the widows and children of those the *Yunusas* of General Abami have gunned down or bombed, you shall surely be avenged. *Exodus 22:22* has told you what to do. *'Cry unto him on your plight. He promised to smite him and he will surely do. "*

The story was the lead in most of the papers the next day. Bishop Lubaba again! What a courage to confront the devil without holding even a razor. The conclusion was simple; he may be marked down like a Luwum this time, as the General may not want to leave anything to chances in view of the impending elections. There, he would be leading six parties to victory at the same time, in an election where no one party would lose and no one party would win. In actual fact, they were no parties but six scarecrows created by the General, a *Kako General* with a defiant club. And true to form, like a *Kako* in the *Forest of a Thousand Demons*, he had a great fulfilment in doing another man's job, however bloody. He perceived every object and shadow as a gnome trying to obstruct his journey of fate to the *Langbodo Eldorado*. Such people he must immediately tackle and dispatch to the great beyond. For General Abami, his own *Kako* club ranged from frame-ups, inhuman detentions and tortures to assassinations and bombings. If Baguludu created thrée parties and did not want any of them to win the election, General Abami created his own to win six victories with six mischiefs in his heart of stone.

He made men weary but he did not succeed in his attempts to weary God. An ungrateful mortal who failed to know that amongst animals, only Man wears the crown ordained to be used for the welfare and the well-being of the people and to adulate the Almighty God, the giver. To him, intellectualism is rubbish, professionalism is nothing, political knowledge is stupid and foolish acquisition, while economic theories are mere exercises to literally impress. If the guns boom and the bombs roar, then all is well and the entire nation and even the world can go to hell. He went to nowhere, knew nothing and cherished no decency. He was the head of state who generated more negative history than any one before him, destroying the civil service by replacing systematic excellence with rat races and undocumented decisions involving life and the fraudulent disbursement of billions.

Hurriedly posted civil servants to the new capital, following his orders, lost virtue and decency. Many homes collapsed as a result of loneliness, lack of accommodation and want, occasioning temptation. Morality was in abeyance while immorality gave out stench, right to the threshold of the *Villa*. The *Villa* became the headquarters of the various slaughter houses in Amuta, the dull but neat and trim city with gothic architectures. Houses sprang up daily with massive mirrors used to panel off concrete walls, windows and doors. General Abami brought wealth to a few and ruins to many, separation to homes, collapse to marriages, whoredom to the young, stress to the old and liquidation to businesses.

*   *   *

The chief security officer to the military head of state and civilian president-in-waiting brought a copy of the *Daily Mirror* to him at the coffee room of the *Villa*. It was almost 1.00p.m and the General was still not ready for office, having received business associates, who daily milked the treasury, till the wee hours of the morning. He ran his government in the night.

"*Morn, Sir*", he threw a sharp salute at the yet to be elected president-in-waiting.

"*Yes, how you dey?*"

"*I dey fine, Sir. This bishop wey no dey read bible but na only newspaper he dey read, don come again o!*

"Lubaba?"

"Yes, Sir. He used very bad words on you at the Bishop's Conference yesterday. Mad president, usurper, coup expert, illiterate general, murderer, devilish strategist, inhuman, stone-faced, dare-devil and so on. Sir, I think he must pay for this one. Can I add him to the list with

Yunusa? This man must choose between preaching and perishing? Enough must be enough, Sir."

"Colonel", the head of state cuts-in.

"These people are over-pampered. The bishop is one of the people we will deal with after I am sworn-in as president. Baguludu didn't win election before he called himself president. He was foolish. I know what I am doing. You just wait until I become president. We can't do anything now as the election is close, but we can also do something. After all, his cousin is a serving officer of the rank of a colonel. We have advised him to call the Bishop to order but he has refused. Get him framed-up as one of the coup suspects and arraign him before the tribunal."

"What of these newspaper boys, Sir?"

"Well, well, leave them alone this time. Already, we have about fifteen of them in either jail or detention. By the time I am president, some will come to the state house to cover a story and disappear forever. They are so easy for me to deal with. If I can depose kings, detain a valid president, devalue notable politicians, dismiss some untouchables, organise a rally of ten million youths, and I am, *Insha Allahu*, today the sole candidate of my own six created political parties, then leave them for me. I am an illiterate, but I am the head of state, ruling those with countless degrees. I pity these people.

"Jimoh, get your papers to my table for signature by Monday morning, under the miscellaneous offences decree. Anyone found to be clandestinely or expressly opposed to this administration would go on leave."

Another order was to be carried out to further enslave the people in the bristle garden of a mad General. The regime of General Abami was full of chaotic advances, retreats and skirmishes. It was a battle no military head fought before and no one would wish to fight again. A violently deceptive regime, the general coerced people to believe that it was behaving splendidly by increasing weakness and worry at home while exhibiting a highly detestable diplomatic gangsterism abroad. Some students were shot dead for demonstrating and consequently causing severe damage to pipelines carrying crude oil to one of the refineries.

It was a national horror that chilled every blood as it was later shown on television. His foreign minister, who attended a world conference on human rights violation few days later was confronted by the foreign press during lunch.

"I am not here to discuss the death of vagabonds' who destroy pipelines and waste national wealth. You think I would have been here if my *estacode* were not ready? We sell our oil to make money to feed the people. I am sorry, let me eat," he guffawed as his jaws ground the rice and chicken for a good mix.

There was a silent but collective consciousness about the misrule of one man highly talented in devilish affinities and who created everything by himself and for himself. The people were carrots and he actually had great carrot salad festivals of them.

He regularly engaged and disengaged them like skewed meat from the oven. The national treasury was also his personal vault that was constantly looted. It took quite a time before the people knew that most of the time he disappeared from the public, he was appearing with new sacks at the treasury. What General Abami did not know about looting is not worth knowing at all. Very ancient and plastic in his wild talents, he was one of a kind who, without a normal qualification, led a revolt in favour of corruption, succeeded with it and became a master of the game.

Orders for detention, trials, torture, and restriction made the nation a skeleton of her old self. The first to nearly actualise a rival theory in military takeovers, General Abami ran an administration that was a paranormal equivalent of a nuclear explosion, which did no one any good. An evil genius in the art of mass hallucination, his excitement, terror and intoxication are not easily identifiable. He omitted no humiliation, he merely piled and timed them to explode at the time he must have gone on leave, which he thought, would be quite some time.

He changed the pages of history by undoing so many deeds of noble men. He nibbled at anything as long as his accounts were full. His agents successfully cornered all worthy and unworthy projects and contracts conceived and awarded in the night, arriving late at international conferences the next day in lipsticks to conceal his failing health. People first saw him as a cardboard villain that would fade off when the other side of the pencil set out to work, but he proved to be a modern day destroyer who hunted his people and nation to near dismemberment.

A strong 'weak' man like the biblical Samson, but unlike Samson who *did it* and still had strength to carry away the massive gate of Gaza, General Abami was carried away through the gates of the *Rocky Villa*, having died the way he lived. His attempt to impose a new form of slavery upon a race set free by God, failed. General Abami wanted to analyse God to those who know God better than him in form, shape and power, without contemplating the consuming power of the Almighty on those who flout his commandments. The change, which he thought he conquered to permanently put himself on the stage, re-asserted itself and conquered him.

The church bells chimed and the monstrous speakers from the minarets on the mosques blared and the people were avenged. Answer to prayers came in a violent torrent that left no room for sympathies. By the breath of His nostrils, he was consumed.

The papers that he ordered were actually prepared but before they could be signed, the state house ambulance zoomed-out of the villa with his *grass*. The casket was full of grass as prophesied by Prophet Isaiah that: *all flesh is grass*. General Sunday Abami went on leave without gun salutes and epitaphs. God avenged his people to end another season of orders; a season when motions were tabled and forcefully adopted, but thank God the house did not adjourn.

Rather, the ugly realities of the landlords as they exchanged the batons frequently used to club their tenants, became frightful stories, of how the neglected became a new landlord and the rightful owner of a meal was served with a coloured killer-starter. How the opportune landlord fingered-off the treasures of his tenants, enjoying a meal of buffalo and caring less about who the poacher was. How the restless minds, thirsty for democracy, pooled resources to force the men of amour to sheath their swords, are meant for another chapter in the history book of a nation endowed, but yet to rise as entreated daily in the national anthem. God avenged his people; a group of compatriots yet to arise!

teaser apocalypse

"... and a contrite heart thou will not despise"
The Psalmist

"We have been accused of extortion and brutalisation in the discharge of our duty. You have to be careful henceforth in performing your duties. Be cautious, ours is to safeguard our nation's integrity and the lives and properties of everyone. As you go back to the barracks... dedicate yourselves to face your professional duties.

We will revive professionalism and training. Societal ills are caused by Nigerians and since the military and the police are also Nigerians, it is only in that regard that blame can be apportioned to them."

General Abdulsalami Abubakar
Former Head of State, addressing military
officers, on 20th August, 1998 in Kaduna.

"a season of orders" is a political satire that exposes the misdemeanour of the fifteen years of military dictatorship in Nigeria and its implications on the civil society.

The book explicitly presents the dictatorial military governments that were hell bent on destroying the people they were supposed to protect. The regimes crippled the economy, bastardized the educational system, and invalidated all social, moral and democratic values.

However, can we blame the military alone for all these social maladies? What about the so-called crusaders of social reforms that were busy scrambling for political appointments and fat contracts or the press that allowed itself to be blindfolded by *egunje* and thus renounced its professional ethics and became the manufacturer of misinformation.

This literary work is highly informative, elegant and revealing. It is indeed a note of lesson containing tutorials for all. The general public will find the book very useful.

About the Author

Prince David Ajisafe Adewumi *(HC, JP)* hails from Ijesa-Isu Ekiti, Ekiti State. He was trained as a journalist at the Institute of Journalism, Lagos. He later studied International Relations at the University of Ife (now Obafemi Awolowo University). He worked at the *Nigerian Tribune* as a reporter and later City Editor for Akure before he joined the pioneering team and founders of Ondo Radio. He was the first Principal Editor Reportorial of Ondo State Television and First Controller News, Radio Nigeria, Akure.

At the closure of the state Federal Radio Corporation of Nigeria (FRCN) stations in 1984, he was redeployed to FRCN Ibadan as Controller News and later to Lagos as Controller FRCN Liaison Office with accreditation to Dodan Barracks in 1990. He finally withdrew his services from the FRCN in 1994 and became the Managing Director of Image Vision Ltd; an image consultancy and advertising outfit. Widely travelled, he was Director General of the Nigeria/Polish Chamber of Commerce in 1993 and has been functioning as Executive Secretary of the Nigerian-Hungarian Chamber of Commerce since its inception in 1995. He was Chairman of the Ekiti State Tourism Board.

In 2002, the Hungarian Government appointed him Honorary Consul for the Republic of Hungary in Lagos. He is the author of the following works: *Terrorist Groups as Actors in International Politics, Points of Disorder, Matrimonial Misfortunes* and the *Biblical Basis for Widowhood Compassion*. He is married with children.

An insight into the military way of thinking in a military-led country for fifteen-years and for which, no one must forget, the civilian society was responsible. Without the co-operation of politicians, technocrats and scholars, the military could not have kept power for so long. This is the secret and the essence that the author has professionally introduced and characterised.

Dr. Janos Balassa
Former Ambassador, the Republic of Hungary.

It's a dramatic expose on ugly realities in the country, delivered in the bloodiest lingua franca. A fictionalized history, it bleaches the green uniform, stains the white 'agbada' and zooms the mind's eyes beyond these barriers.

Smart Ariwodo
Journalist.

This well–written book has graphically captured the gross abuse of power in the soiled hands of little tyrants that seized several African countries and toyed with the lives of African peoples until very recently.

Femi Falana
Lagos.